VANITY RULES

A HISTORY OF AMERICAN FASHION AND BEAUTY

DOROTHY AND THOMAS HOOBLER

Twenty-First Century Books
Brookfield, Connecticut

ACKNOWLEDGMENTS

Our thanks to Cathy Grosfils and Marianne Carter at Colonial Willamsburg; Larry Schwartz, Peter Rohowsky, and John Crino at Archive Photos; Nicole Wells of the New-York Historical Society; Peter Tomlinson of Culver Pictures; Linda J. Ritter of Brown Brothers; Norman Currie at Corbis Bettmann; Anne Esterling of the Museum of the City of New York; Kristin Eshelman of the Spencer Research Library at the University of Kansas; and Merrill Roberts. We particularly want to express our appreciation to our editor, Amy Shields, whose judgment and support were as always a great help in producing this book.

Published by Twenty-First Century Books
A Division of The Millbrook Press, Inc.
2 Old New Milford Road, Brookfield, CT 06804
www.millbrookpress.com

Photographs courtesy of: Archive Photos: 56, 92, 97, 101, 109, 111, 128, 133, 146, 151, 152; Brown Brothers: 77; Byron Collection, Museum of the City of New York: 64; Colonial Williamsburg Foundation: 12, 15, 24; Courtesy, Colorado Historical Society (W-294): 63; Corbis Bettmann: 43, 48, 51, 60, 94, 115; Culver Pictures: 46, 65, 91, 103; Library of Congress: 42; Collection of the New-York Historical Society: 18, 19; Astor, Lenox, and Tilden Foundation, New York Public Library: 34, 41; The Granger Collection: p. 72; Ohlinger: 80, 89, 120, 125, 139; Joseph J. Pennell Collection, Kansas Collection, University of Kansas Libraries: 61; Merrill Roberts: 117; Steve Schapiro: 135; Worcester Art Museum: 28.

Library of Congress Cataloging-in-Publication Data
Hoobler, Dorothy.
Vanity rules : a history of American fashion and beauty / Dorothy and Thomas Hoobler.
p. cm.
Includes bibliographical references (p.)and index.
Summary: Describes the shifting ideal of beauty in the United States, from colonial times to the present, and how it influenced and was influenced by societal and economic changes.
ISBN 0-7613-1258-7 (lib. bdg.)
1. Costume—United States—History Juvenile literature. 2. Fashion—United States—History Juvenile literature. 3. Beauty, Personal—United States—History Juvenile literature. 4. Feminine beauty (Aesthetics)—United States—History Juvenile literature. 5. United States—Social life and customs Juvenile literature. [1. Costume—History. 2. Fashion—History. 3. Beauty, Personal—History. 4. United States—Social life and customs.]
I. Hoobler, Thomas. II. Title.
GT605.H75 2000 391'.00973—dc21 99-12820 CIP

CONTENTS

ᔧ

Introduction
Mirror, Mirror on the Wall . . . 7

1 The Search for Beauty in Colonial America 9

2 Style in the Revolution and Afterward 21

3 Petticoats and Crinolines 31

4 Beauty in an Age of Excess 45

5 The Gibson Girl to the Christy Girl 58

6 The Flapper 73

7 The Glamour Girl 84

8 The New Look 96

9 The Beautiful People 107

10 Power Suits and Disco Wear 121

11 Fitness Is Everything 130

12 Everyone Can Be Beautiful 141

Source Notes 154
Index 157

VANITY RULES

༄

MIRROR, MIRROR ON THE WALL . . .

The stepmother in *Snow White* asks her magic mirror: "Who's the fairest of us all?" When the mirror replies that she is the fairest, her fondest wish is fulfilled. But when it answers, "Snow White," the stepmother is filled with such rage that she determines to kill the girl. In the tale, Snow White's beauty wins the day when the handsome prince kisses her and brings her back to life.

The word *beauty* comes from the Latin *bellus*, meaning "good." In fairy tales, beauty often equals goodness. Cinderella is as beautiful and good as her evil stepsisters are ugly and mean. She catches the handsome prince because she is beautiful. (And he in turn wouldn't be desirable unless he were handsome.)

Beauty may be only skin deep, but your appearance is the first thing you display to others. Our lives are shaped by our looks and the way other people see us. Nancy Friday, who has written about beauty, noted, "None of us escapes the influence that our looks have had on our lives."

Beautiful people are more likely to be popular, and more likely to be successful romantically. But beauty can lead to success in other areas besides romance. Attractive people often have higher self-esteem that enables them to succeed. Self-esteem also leads to a more pleasing personality. Studies have shown that teachers tend to favor more attractive children, and even to believe they are brighter than the less handsome or less beautiful ones.

Yet beauty has a dark side. Beauty can arouse very destructive emotions. It attracts envy, often pitting one woman against another in the competition to attract men. The pursuit of beauty often discourages other kinds of achievement, and it can be very frustrating—for after all, not everybody can be beautiful.

Nancy Friday summed up the damage fostered by the emphasis on beauty: "Beauty has become what our lives are about, not the clothes and seasonal fashions, but the rage, grief, a terrible sense of isolation that we get when we don't get back any good feeling from the money and time we invest in appearance. Appearance is everything, appearance is empty. It's a miserable cheat, this mirror today in which we look nice and feel hollow."

Nevertheless, the beauty business has been an important part of American life since colonial times. Throughout history Americans have used clothing, ornaments, scents, coloring, and decorations to heighten their beauty. They have exercised, dieted, and undergone surgery to make their bodies more attractive. Men were often as eager as women to enhance their beauty. American men have worn wigs, used makeup, and even stuffed their coats and stockings to achieve a more manly look.

No expense was too high and no effort was too great to achieve the beauty ideal. There were decades when women wanted so badly to have a tiny waist that they bound themselves in corsets that almost kept them from breathing. Today men and women pay thousands of dollars for operations that may threaten their health.

Standards of beauty and fashion are continually changing. What accounts for the changes? Sometimes prominent men and women created a look that others tried to imitate. They exerted the same influence in their day as supermodels and celebrities do today. Beauty styles sometimes came from the fact that young people wanted to look different from their elders. (The "hair wars" that pitted young against old began in the seventeenth century.) But styles have also been influenced by wars, changes in the economy, women's demands for equal rights, and even health concerns. The only constant is that people will pay almost any price to be beautiful. Vanity rules!

1

THE SEARCH FOR BEAUTY
IN COLONIAL AMERICA

 The beauty business got started almost as soon as European colonists came face-to-face with Native Americans. People of two very different cultures regarded each other with surprise and curiosity. George Percy of Jamestown described the Native Americans he saw in 1607: "Some paint their bodies black, some red, with artificial knots of sundry lively colors, very beautiful and pleasing to the eye."

The Native Americans knew a lot about dyes and pigments. They did not just apply paint to their bare skin; underneath they smeared a layer of grease or animal fat. Thus was born the first great American cosmetics discovery—foundation cream. The grease enhanced the color and eased the process of removing the paint. In addition, it protected against the cold of winter and insects in summer. Europeans had known of the use of grease or cold cream (originally discovered in classical times by the Greek physician Galen). But they had used it for softening the skin, or sometimes as a lightener, not as a foundation for other cosmetics.

Native Americans had an influence on European fashions as well. Beaver hats became stylish for men in Europe and remained so for over two centuries. Trade in beaver pelts became the first American beauty business among the colonists, and the fur trade was the incentive for later exploration by French, British, and Dutch settlers.

Many Native American contributions have had an impact on fashion history down to the present day. French trappers in northern New York described an unusual hairstyle among the natives. They shaved their heads, leaving only a ridge of hair from forehead to the nape of the neck. It was the Native Americans' custom to make this hair strip stand up by treating it with bear grease. This "Mohawk" hairstyle has been sported by young people in the United States in recent decades.

Native Americans practiced tattooing and body piercing. Some had rings through their noses, the rims of their ears, and other parts of the body. All this has become cutting-edge fashion today, but young people of the late 1990s still haven't quite caught up with seventeenth-century Americans. Those seen by the English at Jamestown strung larger objects through their earlobes—including chicken legs or claws, and even colorful live snakes.

Even though the first English settlers at Jamestown in 1607 were all men, they went to great lengths to improve their appearance. These early Virginians padded their chests with *bombast*, a mixture of rags, horsehair, cotton, and bran. The bombast made their chests appear larger (hence our modern word *bombastic*, used to describe boastful language or behavior). Bombast also offered some protection against the slashes of knives or swords in a fight, although it added about five or six pounds to the jacket, making the wearer somewhat less nimble.

Men also filled their breeches with bombast, sometimes with unusual effects. One popular style was called pumpkin breeches, because they were shaped like the vegetable. Breeches ended just around the knee, so big, bombastic thighs (and buttocks) tended to make the calves appear slim and shapely. Men commonly wore hose (stockings) to further highlight their lower legs.

A problem with bombast was that tears in the fabric left the wearer trailing cereal behind him. The bran in the bombast also attracted lice, and the material could in time rot, creating a nasty odor. Still, people thought the style looked good, and that was all that mattered.

Women soon arrived in Jamestown and they too loved to display their finery. They wore long dresses with wide skirts over petticoats, laced bodices over low-cut blouses, capes, and aprons. They covered their hair with caps at all times, even at home.

Indeed, in the greater freedom of the New World, people used style and clothing to raise their social status. John Pory, an early Jamestown official, noted with disapproval that "our cow-keeper on Sundays goes [dressed] in fresh flaming silk, and the wife . . . of a [coal miner] . . . wears her rough beaver hat with a fair pearl hatband and a silken suit."

Such vanity was also frowned on by the Puritans in Massachusetts. Town councils and the General Court of the colony passed *sumptuary laws*, which tried to regulate the styles and value of clothing that people could wear. Through these laws, colonial leaders sought to keep people in their proper places. In 1651, the General Court banned men of "meane condition" from wearing gold and silver lace, fancy buttons, or great boots. Great boots were high boots with widely flaring tops that used large amounts of leather. Similarly, women of "meane condition" were forbidden to wear silk hoods or scarves. "Meane condition" indicated those below a certain economic level. "Meane" men and women were addressed as "goodman" or "goodwoman" or "goodwife." The terms "Mister" and "Mistress" were reserved for those of higher status.

Many men and women disregarded or challenged the sumptuary laws. In 1653, two women of Newbury, Massachusetts, were arrested for wearing silk hoods and scarves. They were released after proving that their husbands were each worth two hundred pounds, the amount of money necessary for wearing silk. And Massachusetts was not the only colony with sumptuary laws. In Connecticut in 1675, thirty-eight women were charged with wearing clothing above their station in life. That same year, thirty young men were arrested for wearing silk and long hair.

Hair! For over three centuries, American hair has created conflict between generations. Hair, worn long or short, or in certain styles, has been used as a personal and sometimes a political

 A barbershop from colonial times was a full-service business. A man could get a shave, have his hair curled, or his wig touched up.

statement. That was true in Puritan Massachusetts, where people followed the lead of their fellow Puritans in England.

The English Puritans fought against the supporters of the king, Charles I. Royal supporters, called Cavaliers, wore their hair long and curled. Often they also sported a thin mustache and neatly cropped beard, like the king himself. The Puritans, by contrast, shaved their faces and wore their hair short with so little style that it looked like it had been cut with a bowl placed on top of the head. This style gained them the nickname Roundheads.

In 1634 the Massachusetts legislature, dominated by Puritans, passed a law forbidding long hair. Fifteen years later, Governor John Endicott wanted even stricter laws enacted. He and others issued a manifesto declaring their "detestation against the wearing of such long hair, as against a thing uncivil and unmanly, whereby men do deform themselves." Many of those who sported long hair were students at Harvard College. Thus, the long-hair controversy became a youth-versus-age issue.

The next style setter for men was the English king Charles II. Before he came to the throne in 1660, he had lived at the court of the French king Louis XIV. Charles brought back all the latest fashions from France, and naturally they made their way to the English colonies. Wigs now replaced natural hair.

Planters in the southern colonies, who tended to be more fashionable than the staid colonists in New England, were quick to adopt the wig for everyday use. Up north, wigs were considered another of the devil's wiles. The preacher Increase Mather told his congregation that wigs were "horrid Bushes of Vanity."

But the appeal of wigs was just too great. Increase Mather's son, Cotton, appeared before his own congregation wearing a wig. By the end of the seventeenth century, wig wearing was a must for every colonial man who could afford one. They remained in fashion for the eighteenth century as well. (A few individualists resisted the trend—like young Thomas Jefferson, who refused to cover his red hair with a wig until he was elected a member of the Virginia legislature.)

Wigs came in many varieties. The most expensive were made of human hair. Others were made of goat or horsehair. One style was the full-bottomed wig. It had dozens of cascading curls that fell as low as the wearer's waist. Soldiers wore straight-haired wigs with pigtails that they stiffened with clay or tar. Men shaved their heads or cut their hair very short so the wigs would fit. This led to the introduction of the nightcap, to keep the head warm at night. Wigs were placed on a stand while the owner slept, so they would keep their shape.

By the end of the seventeenth century, applying powder to the wigs became fashionable. The purpose was to make them smell better and look cleaner. But it was a lot of trouble. Some people went to barbers to have their wigs powdered. Very wealthy families set aside a special room in their homes for the process. In this *powder room* (the origin of the term used for a room where women fix their makeup today) the man covered his body from the neck down. He also placed a paper or glass cone over his face to keep the powder from suffocating him. A servant or barber would first grease the wig and then shake a bag of powder over it. It was usually flour, but the rich often scented it or tinted it blue or violet.

While men were adopting wigs, women's fashion decreed a hairstyle called the *commode*. This very high style was built up over a wire frame covered with linen, which rose as much as a foot above the face. The woman piled her hair on this construction and arranged it in curls in the latest styles. Some women dyed their hair with saffron to lighten the color. A servant or relative dusted the hair with scented powder, and the concoction was "set" further with perfumed goo made from animal fat or a cream.

As the colonies grew and prospered, women who could afford to be fashionable followed the latest styles from Europe. Ordinarily, they learned about these from people who arrived by ship. Virginia planters often arranged with London merchants to send the latest styles across the Atlantic on ships that had carried Virginia's tobacco crop to England. Martha Washington had a mannequin of her body in a London dress shop so her dresses could be tailored to her exact size. She received dresses in the latest fashion, but made from cheap material. A local Virginia dressmaker could then make up dresses in material that she selected from his stock.

As clothing and millinery (hat) stores opened in the colonial cities, some advertised their wares with *fashion babies*. These were dolls from England or France, dressed in the latest fashions. Usually, the dolls were about two feet high and their hair was also set in the current styles. A Boston seamstress advertised in a 1733 newspaper: "To be seen at Hannah Teatts . . . a Baby drest after the Newest Fashion of Mantues [dresses] and Night Gowns & everything belonging to a dress. . . . Any ladies that desire to see it may either come or send, she will be ready to wait on 'em."

The favored "look" for colonial women was a silhouette that was a gentle curved line. To achieve this, women started with a laced corset. Women had been wearing corsets since the *Mayflower* first landed in 1620. Even young girls dressed in corsets as soon as they could walk, for the whalebone stiffeners in the garment were believed to encourage good posture.

Over the corset women wore a tight-fitting bodice, or top. Attached to the bodice was a triangle of stiff material called a *stomacher*. The stomacher was sometimes stiffened with whalebone or ivory stays. It pressed down everything from breasts to stomach and made it difficult to bend over or even to breathe. Women who wanted to emphasize their breasts used a *bosom friend*, which pushed up and sometimes padded the breasts.

The hottest fashion for women in the first half of the 1700s was the hoop skirt. A frame beneath the skirt set the fabric into a particular shape, which varied according to style. There was the "roundtable" style, the "bell" style, a "gondola" style, and an oval-shaped "elbow" style.

Most outlandish of all was the "pannier" style. A pannier is the yokelike frame that fits over a donkey's back to enable it to carry burdens. The pannier skirt looked like that: It extended straight out either side a *lot*—some were as wide as two feet on each side! That made moving around pretty awkward. Special chairs were made to allow ladies to sit, and doorways were widened so that women could move from room to room. One enterprising inventor developed a pannier hoop that collapsed so that women could pass through a doorway and then expand it.

Men had their ridiculous fashions too. Stylish men of the 1660s wore "petticoat breeches." These had legs trimmed with elaborate lace, ribbons, bows, and embroidery. They were as big and wide as the latest in the raver jeans of the 1990s. Some were as much as five feet around each leg.

In general, men's clothing of the colonial period was as colorful and elaborate as that of women. Suits were made of silks and brocades. Clothing was padded to get the right silhouette. The long coats were often weighted at the hem so they fell "just so." Breeches stopped at the knee, and gentlemen covered their calves with hosiery. A shapely calf was a masculine ideal. It was not unusual for a man to spend more for his hose, which came in many colors, than for his coat. The stockings could be padded if the wearer didn't have naturally shapely legs. Men wore shoes and boots with high heels to further emphasize their legs. Some men's heels of the

The fashion baby provided colonial Americans a look at the newest fashions from England and France. This 23 ½-inch-tall doll is wearing the look for 1770—a silk sacque gown with a stomacher front and the skirt drawn up in "polonaise" fashion, as was the rage in France.

eighteenth century were almost six inches high. Red heels were reserved for the aristocracy.

Cosmetics were freely used in colonial America. In the seventeenth century, the colonial legislature of New Jersey passed a law limiting many beauty aids: "All women, of whatever age, rank, profession or degree, whether virgins, maids or widows, who impose upon, seduce, or betray into matrimony any of his Majesty's subjects by virtue of scents, cosmetics, washes, paints, artificial teeth, false hair or high-heeled shoes, shall incur the penalty of the law now in force against witchcraft."

Men too were heavy users of makeup of all kinds. Most cosmetics were homemade concoctions. Women bought the materials at spice shops or chemists (drugstores) and brewed them from recipes in books or family traditions.

Gerard's Herbal, a manual published in 1633, offered a cure for pimples. It advised the sufferer to eat cucumbers, mixed with oatmeal and mutton, for three weeks. In addition, the person should wash his or her face with a mixture of vinegar, orrice roots, brimstone, camphor, almonds, apples, and juice of lemons. (If it had really worked, teenagers today would still be using it.)

A white complexion with rosy cheeks was the beauty standard for Europeans of the time. To attain this, women rubbed many kinds of store-bought or homemade compounds on their skin. Soliman's Water was a well-known brand name from the 1500s to the 1700s. Women used it to eliminate spots, freckles, and warts. It undoubtedly worked, for the chief ingredient was a compound of mercury that eventually burned off the outer layer of skin.

Colonial women realized that the sun darkened their complexions. To protect their skin, many wore masks when they went outside. These "sun-expelling" masks came in many colors and were worn by children as well as adults. George Washington ordered some from England for his wife, Martha, and his stepdaughter. Sometimes wearers held the masks in place by an attached handle. But others were fitted with a silver mouthpiece so they could be worn while riding a horse. The wearer bit down on the mouthpiece to keep the mask in place.

Both men and women used red lipstick and green or blue coloring on their eyelids. These were all made from vegetable dyes, such as beets. Men carried mirrors inside their hats to check on their looks; women concealed mirrors in little snuffboxes. Rouge was available as Spanish paper, Spanish felt, or Spanish wool. Each of these substances was saturated with red dye. Women and men rubbed them onto dampened cheeks to achieve a rosy glow. False eyebrows were often made of mouse skin. At other times, it was fashionable to darken the natural eyebrows with a lead comb.

In an era when people regarded baths as unhealthy, perfumes were an absolute necessity for both sexes. Perfume was applied to the hair as well as the clothing. It usually came not in liquid form, but as a paste or gel. People carried the paste in small boxes or bags (called *pomanders*) when they went outside. The scent of real flowers also helped mask body odors. When wearing a corsage at a ball, women pinned bosom bottles (filled with water or perfume) to their dresses so the flowers would stay fresh.

Perfumes were either home concoctions or purchased from a chemist. In 1752, Dr. William Hunter, an English physician, opened a shop in Newport, Rhode Island. This was the origin of the Caswell-Massey Company, which today claims to be "the oldest chemists and perfumers in America." The company still produces its Number Six cologne from the original colonial formula.

Perfumers also sold gloves made of chicken skin that were filled with sweet-smelling substances such as almond paste or flowers, and meant to be worn in bed overnight. Similar gloves, sometimes of dog skin, were filled with oils to smooth wrinkled hands.

Having beautiful teeth was always a problem, for dental care was limited to pulling teeth that were too painful to endure. People cleaned their teeth with honey and sugar(!); crushed bone mixed with fruit peel; or burned alum mixed with ground rosemary. The colonists didn't have toothbrushes, but used coarse linen tooth cloths. Stains on the teeth were removed by rubbing them with a pumice stone. Tooth decay leads to bad breath, so people used mouthwashes to kill the odor. *Gerard's Herbal* recommended water mixed with rosemary, cloves, mace, cinnamon, and anise seed.

THE CROSS-DRESSING GOVERNOR

Today, the entertainer RuPaul is well known as a cross-dresser—a man who wears women's clothing. For centuries there have been some men who have secretly enjoyed making that king of clothing switch.

In colonial times, a governor of New York publicly appeared in his wife's gowns. This was Edward Hyde, Lord Cornbury, who served as governor from 1702 to 1708.

Lord Cornbury

He was given the post by his cousin, Queen Anne, and one explanation for his cross-dressing is that he intended it as a tribute to the queen. Apparently, he enjoyed displaying himself before the citizens in such garb, complete with rouge and powder. It was reported that he enjoyed strolling around the parapets of the fort he commanded, dressed as a woman.

The governor had a wife and seven young children. His wife, Katherine—herself the daughter of a lord—also scandalized the citizens of New York with her behavior. It was reported that Lord Cornbury married her because he loved the shape of her ears; at their wedding, he kissed her ears instead of her lips to end the ceremony. However, the governor was not a very generous man, and his wife was reduced to borrowing clothing and even housewares from the unfortunate people of New York City, then the colonial capital. According to some stories, when housewives heard her carriage approaching, they hid the silver and chinaware. That didn't deter Lady Cornbury, who sent her servants to ferret out anything worthwhile she had missed on her "visits."

Lady Cornbury died at the age of thirty-four, while her husband was still governor. The following year, he was recalled to England, where the queen continued to entrust him with important responsibilities. Since then, no New York governors (all males) have appeared in public wearing a dress.

In colonial times, plump cheeks were regarded as desirable for a woman. Those who didn't come by them naturally stuffed *plumpers* in their mouths. These were small balls of cork, and were also used to hide the hollows caused by missing teeth.

Plumpers weren't the only artificial way to enhance one's looks. Smallpox, a common disease at that time, left scars on people's faces. And of course people worried about pimples and other blemishes. A fashionable solution was to put a cloth patch over the offending spot. These patches came in fanciful shapes, such as stars or crescents, and were usually black. Gum arabic, something like rubber cement, was used to stick them onto the face.

For those who knew the signals, the location of a patch could send a message. Patches placed at the corners of the eyes were

Collection of The New-York Historical Society (and facing page)

↬ *Beauty patches were a fashion must during the entire colonial period. A poem of the time said of the fashionable lady: "Her patches are of every cut, For pimples and for scars; Here's all the wandering planets' signs, And some of the fixed stars." This print shows women celebrating Washington's Birthday in the nineteenth century by dressing up as their grandmothers did.*

known as "impassioned patches"; those on the cheek were called "gallants." If you placed one on your lips, it was a sign you were available.

Fashions come and go, but you can see that the colonists were just as style conscious and fond of fads as people are today. The only thing that might seem missing from this picture is the modern craze for dieting and exercise. However, Benjamin Franklin covered both of these in his popular *Poor Richard's Almanac*. He advised his readers: "Labour in the first place to bring thy Appetite into Subjection to Reason. The Difficulty lies, in finding out an exact measure; but eat for Necessity, not Pleasure." As he would say today, "Don't overeat!"

2

STYLE IN THE REVOLUTION AND AFTERWARD

 In the years leading up to the American Revolution, two beauty ideals competed for the hearts of citizens. Fashion was linked to politics, as colonists who supported the growing independence movement often favored simpler styles. The Daughters of Liberty, a women's group founded in 1765, pledged to boycott imported English goods. These imports included beauty products such as cosmetics and false hair, as well as clothing. The Daughters of Liberty called on patriot women to spin the cloth for their own garments, rather than use English cloth. Of course, in rural areas and along the frontier, as well as among poorer folk, homespun cloth was the norm. But in towns and cities by 1765, imported English cloth was widely used.

Many women organized spinning, sewing, and knitting bees to help the colonies become economically independent. Throughout New England, the Daughters of Liberty flocked to churches and homes and competed with each other to produce the most "homespun" material. Abigail Foote wrote in her diary: "I carded two pounds of whole wool and felt Nationally."

Some colonists refused to give up English fashion, which at this time went to elaborate extremes. Men who dressed in high style were called "macaronis," after the Macaroni Club, which was founded in London in the 1760s. You could tell a Macaroni member by his enormous wig, which towered a foot or more above his head. In the back, the false hair was twisted into a large queue, or ponytail, that hung down over the shoulders. To emphasize the size of the wig, the Macaroni wore a small hat perched on top.

Also, the young Macaronis wore very, very tight breeches. One gentleman, ordering a pair from his tailor, said, "If I can get into 'em, I won't pay for 'em." Indeed, it was sometimes necessary for a man to hang the breeches on hooks, climb on a stepladder above them, and then lower himself carefully inside.

Coats reflected the peacock attitude. They came in beautiful color combinations such as violet and red, and were often striped and ornamented with large buttons. The front of the jacket was cut sharply toward the sides to show off the shirt beneath. Shirts were decorated with bows and lace collars. Macaronis doused themselves liberally with scent.

Some American colonists who opposed British policies still adopted the Macaroni style. The most prominent was John Hancock, said to be the wealthiest man in the colonies. He used to drive through Boston in his carriage, wearing a crimson coat with gold braid and a sky-blue waistcoat in moiré silk. Hancock's large and fancy signature on the Declaration of Independence tells you he enjoyed showing off.

When the Revolution came, the British soldiers mocked the shabbily dressed colonial army with the song, "Yankee Doodle," including the words, "He stuck a feather in his cap and called it Macaroni." The Patriot soldiers sang it back—with pride—when they defeated the British at the battle of Concord, Massachusetts. Since then, it has been a popular American song, even though few remember the origin of the word *Macaroni.*

Most colonial women, even those who supported independence, wanted to be in fashion if they could. To help the style-conscious, a new publication called *The Ladies Magazine* began appearing in 1770. Published in London, it circulated throughout the colonies. It was the first magazine to print engraved pictures of styles. Printers call engravings "plates," and from this magazine comes the term *fashion plate*—which today means someone who is very current in style.

Many women adopted extreme hairstyles that came from France. Perhaps they were trying to make up for the dullness of their homespun clothing by flaunting their hair. From the 1750s hairstyles began to get higher and higher. At that time, Madame Pompadour, the beautiful mistress of the French king Louis XV, wore her hair high at the front without a part. This style became known as the *pompadour*.

In the 1770s women's hair was swept up to the highest levels ever—sometimes more than a foot high. Hairdressers flourished, for only a professional could create these styles, and it often took a full day to complete them. The hairdresser used as a base a large pad (called a *heddus roll*) stuffed with horsehair, wool, bran, straw, or even rope. To sculpt the hair over the roll, the hairdresser soaked it with a paste made of flour and water. It might have been greased as well. Decorations such as bows, flowers, and feathers gave a final touch of beauty. Some women carried the style to its limit by adding special objects—model ships, flags, carved scenery—to create an elaborate tableau, or scene, on the tops of their heads.

Remember, this was not a wig and couldn't be removed unless you wanted to sit down and do it all over again the next day. Once in place, these elaborate coiffures had to last for weeks. Women bought long-handled sticks with hooked ends so they could poke them into the hair to scratch their heads. And the heads *needed* scratching, for fleas, lice, roaches, and other live creatures would sometimes nest in the maze of hair. Women slept with their necks on wooden supports so that the hairdo wouldn't be ruined. Because the style was so high, doorways had to be raised, and some women couldn't sit upright in closed carriages.

Children wore these monster hairstyles too. In 1770, eleven-year-old Anna Green Winslow wrote in her diary: "I had my HEDDUS roll [put] on; Aunt Storer said it ought to be made less, Aunt Deming said it ought not to be made at all. It makes my head itch and ache and burn like anything. . . . *This* famous roll is not made *wholly* of a red *Cow Tail*, but is a mixture of that & horsehair (very coarse) & a little human hair of a yellow hue that I suppose was taken out of the back part of an old wig."

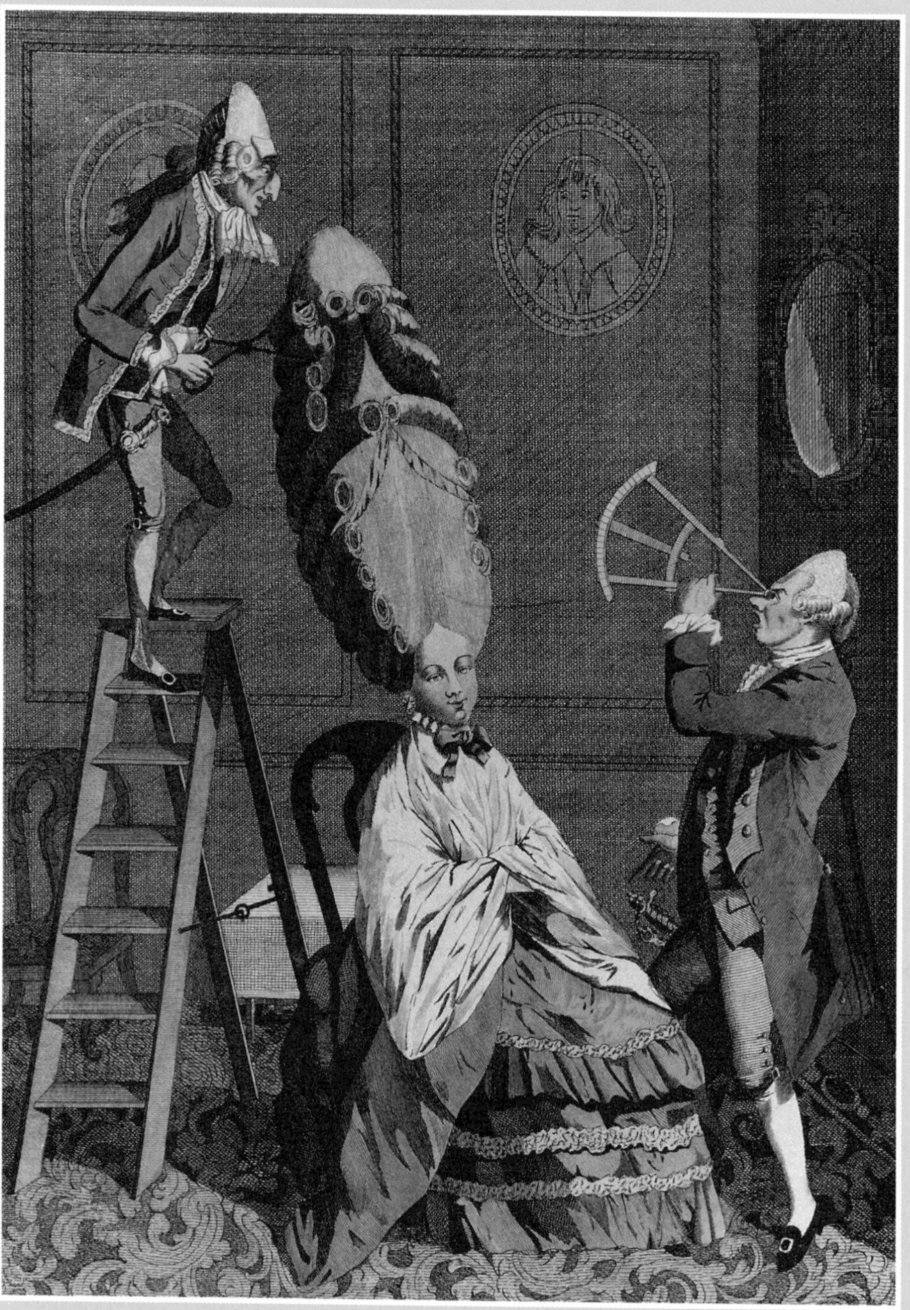

The 1770s saw the styling of women's hair reach ridiculous heights. Although this picture exaggerates, many women actually had trouble getting through doors or into carriages because they wore their hair so high.

Once the Revolution started in 1775, staying in fashion became more difficult. Ships from Britain now carried soldiers and weapons. There was no need for a boycott of British goods—they were no longer available. Fancy dress items disappeared rapidly. No more patches, powders, hoops, petticoats, fancy high-heeled shoes, or heddus rolls. Only in cities like New York and Philadelphia, which were occupied by the British, did the social whirl of grand parties and balls continue.

Washington insisted that each man in his army "shave, have clean hands, and a general air of neatness." He imposed a penalty of five lashes on any soldier whose hat was carelessly unlooped or uncocked. (A cocked hat had its brim turned up in three places, held up with a loop and button.) Few soldiers wore wigs; Washington himself did not while serving in the army. He ordered that the men keep their hair combed and powdered. Most men let their hair grow long and tied it in queues with a ribbon.

Among civilians, fashion remained important as a patriotic gesture. Many women sported a hairdo with thirteen rolls to show their support for the now-independent thirteen states. Attacks on British style were popular. After the colonial troops recaptured Philadelphia in 1778, many celebrated the Fourth of July with special joy. Elizabeth Drinker noted in her diary that there was "a very high Head dress…exhibited thro the Streets this afternoon on a very dirty Woman with a mob after her, with Drums &tc. by way of ridiculing that very foolish fashion."

Meanwhile, Benjamin Franklin used his diplomatic skills in Paris, persuading the French to lend aid to the colonists. Franklin had taken along formal clothing to wear at court, but on his arrival discovered it was too small for him. He made the most of the situation by going to the other extreme: He dressed in plain breeches, shirt, waistcoat, and coonskin cap. The French, always alert to creative fashion trends, were charmed. They regarded Franklin as "the natural man"—a true representative of America.

The colonists won the war and now they were proud citizens of a new nation, a republic. It seemed wrong to imitate the styles of

European aristocrats, and people adopted much simpler looks. Many people showed their American pride by wearing home-grown, handspun, and handmade fashions. The Washingtons, both George and Martha, appeared in homespun clothing on public occasions, even though they were wealthy. Calico cloth became very popular. Portraits of Washington or Franklin adorned women's dresses, along with Liberty caps and stars and stripes. Red, white, and blue—the colors of the new nation's flag—were in fashion for the clothing of both men and women.

Rouge and false eyebrows went out of fashion, as women stressed the natural look. Instead, women took great care to keep their skin as white as possible. Most women wore bonnets and carried parasols whenever they went outside. Dolley Madison, later a First Lady, remembered that as a girl in Virginia she wore a white linen mask to shield her cheeks from the sun and wind, as well as a bonnet that her mother sewed on her each morning before school. She also wore long gloves to protect her arms and hands.

Not all women followed the fashion of simplicity and plainness. In the cities many wealthy women wanted to parade their style and beauty. A French visitor who dined with the president of the Congress in Philadelphia rather prudishly described his impressions of the women of the new republic. "I saw at his house," the Frenchman wrote, "at dinner, seven or eight women, all dressed in great hats, plumes, &ct. It was with pain that I remarked [noticed] much of pretension in some of these women; one acted the giddy, vivacious; another, the woman of sentiment. . . . Two among them had their bosoms very bared. I was scandalized at this indecency among republicans."

Some women wondered if attitudes toward beauty and fashion should be different in a republic. Some now claimed that teaching girls to dress well should not be such an important part of their upbringing. Hadn't women shown during the struggle against Great Britain that they were capable of a much more substantial role in the new republic? Shouldn't republican women be confident and self-reliant rather than slaves to fashion and beauty standards?

Dr. Benjamin Rush of Philadelphia observed, "I have sometimes been led to ascribe the invention of ridiculous and expensive fashions in female dress entirely to the gentlemen in order to divert the ladies from improving their minds and thereby to secure a more arbitrary and unlimited authority over them." Rush had thus described the age-old dilemma of women—what a modern writer has called "the beauty myth." Women spent so much of their energy seeking beauty that there was little time for other ambitions.

But the republican ideal of the competent and independent woman lost out to the traditional ideal: marriage as a woman's lifetime goal. In the marriage market, beauty and charm counted for more than intelligence and ability. Molly Tilghman of Maryland expressed the feeling in a letter to her cousin, about the relative values of beauty and intelligence. "Wisdom says it [beauty] is a fading flower, but fading as it is, it attracts more admiration than wit, goodness, or anything else in the world." The power of beauty and its role in women's lives remains strong to this day.

Instead of a new role for women, the 1790s saw the start of a new beauty ideal and style. It came from France, inspired by the French Revolution, which had broken out in 1789. The uprising against the privileges of the upper classes—and later against the king—brought an end to aristocratic dress and fashion. French women threw away their corsets and hoops. Both sexes stopped powdering their hair and wearing wigs. Men, to show support for the Revolution, wore the trousers of the workers, or *sans culottes*. The term referred to the fact that they didn't dress in the knee-length breeches of the aristocracy. The French turned to the ancient Greeks and Romans for inspiration and brought forth a more graceful draped look.

The United States welcomed both styles and refugees from France. As the Revolution became more radical and violent, many French citizens fled. Some of them became an important part of the early United States beauty business. They included dressmakers, milliners (hatmakers), seamstresses, and hairdressers. A French name was always attractive to American customers.

One such immigrant, a Monsieur Lefoy, a well-known hairdresser, gave advice to other men who wanted to practice his profession. "He who lives in the boudoir [most hairdressers went to the homes of wealthy clients], whose 'flying fingers' are incessantly revolving around charms [that are] most delicate and bewitching" must be discreet. Lefoy advised developing a manner that was confiding as well as reserved. In addition, he said, careful and witty speech would add to the hairdresser's professional appeal. Monsieur Lefoy would be a popular hairdresser today as well.

In the mid-1790s, American women began to wear narrow, high-waisted dresses, made of light material that hung down in folds, giving just a glimpse of the ankle. The necklines fell as the waistlines rose. A ribbon representing the waist surrounded the body just below the breasts, making them more prominent. Dresses for the daytime had high collars; those for evening wear had ever-lower necklines. These gowns were usually worn with slippers known as "Roman sandals." The high-waisted style became known as *Empire* style, for the period after the French Revolution when Napoleon Bonaparte ruled France as its emperor. The Empire style, with variations, lasted from the mid-1790s to around 1820.

This style was truly revolutionary, a real break with the past. Instead of the layered look of earlier times—with a separate bodice, or top, sleeves, and skirt—now the dress was often a single piece of material. It was drawn together with a string that hung from the shoulders, giving women a different silhouette. Formerly, undergarments such as corsets or hoops shaped the figure. Full skirts covered these styles. In the Empire style, the material of the gown revealed the natural shape of the wearer's body. False bosoms, some made of papier mâché complete with painted nipples, and special corsets that extended to the hips were available to those who wanted the youthful look.

This stylish couple from the early years of the nineteenth century show the revolution in fashion. The lady's dress flows down, showing the gentle curves of her body. If she was slim, a lady could throw out her corset. The man's coat reaches his knees, and the collar on his shirt grazes his ears. Within a few years, his trousers would take on a form more like the pants of today.

A BEAUTY BEST-SELLER

In the 1700s and for centuries before, people passed down recipes (or "receipts") for cosmetics the way they did for food. In 1775 a London publisher brought out *The Toilet of Flora*, a collection of beauty concoctions. (The word *toilet* at that time meant the process of dressing and grooming.) The book's introduction said that it would "point out and explain to the Fair Sex the Methods by which they may preserve and add to their Charms."

The recipes make use of herbs, spices, flowers, and other natural ingredients. However, they are mostly impractical for preparation today. One was for "Imperial Water," which had many uses: "takes away wrinkles and renders the skin extremely delicate; it also whitens the Teeth and abates the toothache, sweetens the breath, and strengthens the gums." Imperial water would certainly improve one's mood, for the recipe began: "Take five quarts of brandy." It recommends adding frankincense, mastic, benjamin, gum arabic, cloves, nutmeg, pine nuts, almonds, and musk.

No book of this kind was complete without recipes for lightening the skin. The author provided "An Admirable Varnish," and the process for making it showed how much time women of that era spent working on such items: "Take equal parts of Lemon Juice, and Whites of new laid Eggs, beat them well together in a glazed earthen pan, which put on a slow fire, and keep the mixture constantly stirring with a wooden spatula, till it has acquired the consistence of soft butter. Keep it for use, and at the time of applying it, add a few drops of any Essence [perfume] you like best."

Critics thought the Empire style was too revealing. Sometimes the dresses were made of semitransparent material with a see-through underchemise. Some women moistened the thin material so that it clung even closer to the figure. In 1801 a Georgia newspaper offered as a joke a prize "to the lady…who shall so arrange her few garments as to appear nearest to naked."

A more natural, shorter hairstyle went along with the Empire dresses. The artificial constructions of the 1770s and 1780s were replaced by patterns of curls around the face. Greater naturalness was the style in cosmetics too. Face powder made of ground rice adorned the faces of the elite. In rural areas, ground-up chalk was used for powder and cut-up beetroot or rose petals used for rouge. Most of all, women wanted to look natural, and cosmetics were not obtrusively used. The fastest growing cosmetic of the time was soap.

Like women, men sought a look with greater naturalness. Patches and masks were dropped. Wigs and powdered hair gave way to a shorter cut in imitation of the style seen on Roman statues. Men exchanged heavy perfume for a light cologne and clean skin. Bathing was in for both sexes.

Benjamin Franklin had written earlier about the relationship of plain clothing to the image of seriousness. He noted in his *Autobiography*: "In order to secure my credit and character as a tradesman, I took care not only to be in reality industrious and frugal, but to avoid all appearance to the contrary. I *drest* plainly." And dressing plainly would be the male fashion for almost two centuries.

From France came the trousers that started to replace breeches for everyday wear after 1800. At the same time, a new style of men's jacket was appearing. Double breasted at first, it soon started to resemble the suit coat that men wear today. Men also started to wear vests, which evolved from the waistcoats of the past. Vests did not at this time match the material of the jacket. All three elements—pants, coat, vest—were made of contrasting material. But the colors of the clothing were dark and muted, no longer bright and vivid. Men wore stiff collars that were high enough to cut into their cheeks.

These changes in the male beauty image are known as "the great renunciation." Before, men had dressed to draw attention to themselves much as women did. They piled on the makeup and wore bright-colored clothing. But in the early 1800s, men gave up their peacock plumage, and not until recent years have they begun to recover it.

3

PETTICOATS AND CRINOLINES

 From 1820 to the Civil War, the United States experienced many changes. Politically, democracy flourished as the right to vote was extended to virtually all white males. Economically, the country became wealthier as the Industrial Revolution took off. These changes affected the beauty industry, and a new beauty ideal arrived.

Around the year 1829 the waistline of fashionable dresses started to fall. By the end of the 1830s, it had reached the natural level. The new look emphasized the waist. Unfortunately for women an eighteen-inch waist was the fashion ideal! Supposedly, that made the waist small enough for a man to encircle it with his hands. At the same time, to accentuate the small waist, both the bodice and the skirt were made wider. Underneath their skirts, women wore layer after layer of petticoats to produce a bell-shaped silhouette.

This new style required elaborate undergarments to artificially shape women's bodies. To achieve the tiny waists, women had to undergo the torture of wearing excruciatingly tight corsets. As more petticoats were added to the skirts, they had to be stiffened at the hems by whalebone or bamboo to keep their shape. The complete woman's outfit became much heavier than a man's suit, and it was exhausting to walk around in it. This style would remain popular for about forty years.

Ironically, fashionable women of the time were expected to appear delicate, frail, thin, and pale. They should be short and slight with sloped shoulders and rounded arms. Slimness, small hands, and small feet supposedly were signs of upper-class breeding. Frances Kemble, an English actress who married an American, wrote that many young women looked as if "a puff of wind would break them in half or a drop of water soak them through." Plumpness was acceptable and expected, however, in married women.

Men too were admired for delicate features and smallness. Napoleon had made shortness manly. Today's brawny ideal—the "jock"—was not attractive in pre-Civil War America. Engravings of the time show fashionable men were wasp-waisted with tiny mouths like their feminine counterparts. Men's fashions accentuated the look with jackets with curved shoulders and small waists. Many men used whalebone stays in their clothing to get the look. One writer said that the ideal man "must not measure more than 24 inches around the chest; his face must be pale, thin, and long; and he must be spindle-shanked [have thin calves]." The same author said: "There is nothing our women dislike so much as corpulency [fatness]." In the late 1820s and 1830s, the slim body even had political significance. With lean Andrew Jackson as president, fat was associated with excessive wealth or fussy aristocrats, who were out of favor at the time.

Probably the most influential figure on style and fashion in this era was the English poet Lord Byron, with his fair skin and delicate features. He was a romantic figure whose dashing exploits added to his fame. Young people copied his dress and style obsessively. Byron kept his hair shiny by applying Macassar oil, which came from the nuts of trees on the Celebes Islands. Macassar oil became so popular in the United States that housewives placed lace doilies on the backs of chairs and sofas to protect them from oily heads. These lacy coverings kept the name *antimacassars* well into the twentieth century.

Because Byron had a tendency to gain weight, he took drastic steps to keep his slim figure. He starved himself, eating little but hard biscuits and soda water, or potatoes soaked in vinegar. Byron also had a negative attitude toward women and food. He found the sight of women eating disgusting. "A woman," he wrote, "should never be seen eating or drinking, unless it is *lobster salad* and *champagne*, the only truly feminine and becoming viands [edibles]." Many women did indeed avoid eating in public places, unless the table was set with those two foods.

The "ideal beauty" of the belle and the beau could be found in lithographs and magazines. Cheap lithographs, or prints—such as those made by Currier and Ives—spread the beauty ideals throughout the United States. The same was true of the illustrations and engravings in magazines, beauty manuals, and etiquette books that became popular at this time. No publication would be as influential as *Godey's Lady's Book*. After Sara Josefa Hale became its editor in 1837, it gained a huge audience.

Hale's editorial policy was to print articles and stories by the best-known authors of the day, such as Nathaniel Hawthorne, Edgar Allan Poe, Henry Wadsworth Longfellow, and Harriet Beecher Stowe, who later wrote *Uncle Tom's Cabin*. Along with these authors, Hale offered her readers colored fashion plates, recipes, beauty and health tips, and other useful advice. *Godey's* had enormous influence. Its circulation reached 100,000 by the Civil War, and subscribers passed it on to friends and neighbors.

Two generations of American women depended on *Godey's* to tell them how they should dress, cook, and act. Engravings showed women posed with their heads to one side and the arms slightly bent, to produce a curved figure—curved was better than straight. Women were advised not even to cross the room in a straight line, but to move in an arc. They were also to bend their arms when lifting anything and to crook the little finger when pouring tea.

Mrs. Hale was firm in her opinions. She introduced the term *lingerie* into English and advised women to wear fine underclothes. Mrs. Hale's opinions prevailed, and fancy underwear became a growing business.

One reason for the success of *Godey's* was that more people than ever before wanted to become fashionable. When Andrew Jackson became president in 1829, it was a triumph for "the common man." Himself from a humble background, Jackson won the

⤷ Godey's Lady's Book *was very influential in the first half of the nineteenth century. Women all over the United States consulted it to learn about fashion. This fashion plate from Godey's pages is from the early 1840s. Notice that the man's coat pinches his waist almost as much as the woman's dress does. And it required many petticoats to get the bell effect of the woman's skirt.*

election with the support of workingmen and small farmers. The era of Jacksonian Democracy had begun.

In Jacksonian America, people of the middle and working classes strived to dress and look well. Catharine Beecher noted: "There are no distinctive classes, as in aristocratic lands. Thus, the person of humble means is brought into contact with those of vast wealth…and [there is] a constant temptation…to imitate the customs, and to strive for the enjoyments of those who possess larger means."

The Industrial Revolution had arrived, and factories produced cloth at a far lower price than it could be made at home. Cloth mills hired women (and children) to work at the mechanized looms, for they had smaller and more nimble fingers for the work. Women who came to mill towns or cities to find jobs lived in boarding-houses. They were spared the chores of housework, and they were earning an income, however meager. Even though they were working class, they wanted to use their free time and money to make themselves fashionable. Many observers noted that American women all dressed the same way, regardless of their station in life. The only differences in their dress were in the quality of material.

Working-class men were not immune to the allure of fashion and looking good. George Sala, a visitor from England, saw that some of the best-dressed American men were hotel clerks. He also noted the popularity of barbershops and hairdressing salons. "Every American who does not wish to be thought 'small potatoes' or a 'ham-fatter' or 'corner-loafer' is carefully 'barbed' and fixed up in a hair dressing saloon every day," reported Sala.

The greater demand for fashionable clothing led to the production of "ready-to-wear" garments for men. With the help of a tape measure, invented around 1820, skilled tailors could turn out fitted suits based on common rules of masculine proportions. Sailors were the first to buy premade garments, because they didn't have time to be measured for a suit and then wait for it to be made before their ship left port. By 1835 ready-to-wear clothing for men was a major industry in New York, Philadelphia, and Boston. The store that would become known as Brooks Brothers was a pioneer in ready-to-wear.

The invention of the sewing machine made the production of clothing even cheaper. It also provided another way for women to take part in the beauty business, for they now could do "piecework" at home. Clothing stores and tailors paid them for making dresses or suits.

And what did they do with the money they earned? Anne Royall, a journalist, noted: "I have known young ladies supporting themselves [to] sit up till twelve o'clock at night, to complete a suit of clothes, the proceeds of which was to purchase a fine cap, or a plume of feather, to deck herself for church. Hundreds of those females thus maintain themselves in a style of splendor; no ladies in the city dress finer."

In 1846 an Irish immigrant shopkeeper, Alexander T. Stewart, opened a huge new store on Broadway in New York City. Called the Marble Dry-Goods Palace (dry goods was a term for cloth and clothing), A. T. Stewart's department store catered to women, offering them everything they needed in the way of clothing and accessories. Previously, women had to visit many different shops to assemble an outfit.

Women's dresses were still elaborately designed and decorated, and so they needed to be hand tailored. But a woman could go to Stewart's and pick out cloth, ribbon, trimmings, and accessories such as umbrellas, hats, and handbags. Stewart's also sold corsets, crinolines, and other undergarments. The customer could have her purchases made into a dress by the stores' own seamstresses, or go to an outside dressmaker.

Stewart was a shrewd retailer. He hired good-looking men dressed in the latest fashions as sales clerks. A manager greeted customers at the door and would assign an employee to help women shop, if they desired. Women enjoyed these personal touches. They also liked the fact that Stewart's set fixed prices for its goods—this meant women did not face the unpleasant prospect of haggling over prices, which they did at almost every other store of the time.

A STORE THAT BECAME A LEGEND

In 1818, Henry Sands Brooks opened a clothing store for men in lower Manhattan. Henry treated his customers well, serving fine liquor to those who shopped there, and wrapping packages in black silk handkerchiefs. He offered ready-made and hand-tailored suits in the finest fabrics available. Brooks himself was known throughout the city as a "dandy" who always dressed in the latest fashion.

The store became Brooks Brothers in 1850 and adopted a sheep as its trademark. For those in the know, the trademark was also the symbol of the Order of the Golden Fleece, a society to which many members of European royalty belonged. By 1858, Brooks Brothers had moved to a larger store on Broadway, which was illuminated by gaslight.

Brooks Brothers became the premier men's clothing store in New York City. Here, Abraham Lincoln bought the overcoat he wore to his second inaugural and the suit that he wore to Ford's Theater on the night he was assassinated. It maintained its reputation, outfitting wealthy and powerful men (and those who aspired to be wealthy or powerful) through most of the twentieth century.

Stewart made it clear that his was a store for women. He sold refreshments, but no liquor (which men's tailor shops served to their customers.) The store had a women's parlor on the second floor, with dozens of full-length mirrors, where women could freshen up and see what they looked like in the store's wares.

Whether you were rich or poor, getting the right "look" required effort. Achieving the eighteen-inch waist also required considerable help. Putting on a corset (or as it was called, an "unmentionable") was a torturous half an hour job. Maids, sisters, and sympathetic husbands were called into service. If all else failed, a young lady would tie the ends of the corset laces around a bedpost and pull away from it.

The corset had to be tightened so much that it could cause fainting and headaches. It restricted a woman's ability to move around, and could cause serious internal damage as well. Corsets probably caused spinal and uterine disorders in many women, as well as broken ribs, constipation, and indigestion.

But at least women of this era were spared the hours-long preparation of complex hairstyles. The fashions were simpler, framing the face with cascading curls and pulling the hair in back into a chignon or bun. Women were advised to brush their hair vigorously to achieve a higher gloss. Some crimped their hair with curling irons heated over a fire. "Hair restorers" were used to color gray hair. Various decorations—feathers, flowers, combs, jewels, ribbons, and gold or silver hair bands—added a touch of style.

In northern cities, African American women wanted beauty products to suit their own needs. African American periodicals advertised hair care products. Beauty parlors operated by and for African Americans also opened. Three sisters—Cecelia Remond Putnam, Marchita Remond, and Caroline Remond—owned the Ladies Hair Work Salon in Salem, Massachusetts, as well as the largest wig factory in the state. The sisters were active in the abolitionist movement and used their profits to support the cause.

The advertisements from both black- and white-owned beauty companies gave the message that European looks were the only acceptable ones. Martin Freeman, writing in the *Anglo-African*

Magazine, pointed out that black children were taught they were pretty only to the degree they resembled "the Anglo-Saxon standard. Hence flat noses must be pinched up. Kinky hair must be subjected to a straightening process…sometimes the natural hair is shaved off and its place supplied by a straight wig. Thick lips are puckered up and drawn in. Beautiful black and brown faces by the application of rouge and lily white powder are made to assume unnatural tints, like the livid hues of painted corpses."

Slaves in the South did not receive beauty images from magazines or lithographs. House servants often copied the hairstyles of the white family members. But other slaves kept African hair traditions alive. They continued to wrap, braid, and cornrow their hair with colored thread in the traditional manner, and covered their hair with a bandanna.

As far as cosmetics went, "naturalness" was still in for everyone. *Godey's Lady's Book* told its readers: "Whatever is false or artificial is as reprehensible in dress as in morals. Pearl powder, and rouge, false and dyed hair, are falsehoods addressed to the eye instead of the ear; and, like other untruths, seldom escape detection and contempt. In spite of the skill with which they are employed, their artificiality is betrayed by their utter want of harmony with the surrounding parts."

Neither rouge nor lipstick was acceptable among respectable women. To achieve the delicate look, women sipped arsenic and other chemicals thought to produce whiter skin. Creams and lotions to improve the skin were also available. In 1846, Theron Pond developed Pond's Extract, the sale of which made his company a leader in the beauty business. Women also used perfumes and colognes, such as rosewater, oil of amber, orris, peppermint, and vanilla.

The desire to attain a thin and delicate look also produced a craze for diets and exercises. Visitors to the United States noted that its citizens were obsessed with weight. Scales were available in public places; those in rural areas weighed themselves at county fairs. David Macrae, from Scotland, noted: "Every girl knows her own weight to within an ounce or two, and is ready to mention it at a moment's notice."

The granddaddy of American diets was the Reverend Sylvester Graham. In the 1830s he lectured on proper eating as a way to good health. He advocated a plain diet that included whole grains, vegetables, and a lot of pure water. Strictly forbidden were coffee, tea, tobacco, and drugs such as opium (which was then the basis for many patent medicines). Graham also criticized the use of spices because he believed they stimulated people to overeat. He invented the Graham cracker as a food that fit his health requirements.

Diocletian Lewis developed the New Gymnastics for exercise classes at a school he founded in Boston in 1861. His program used wooden rings, dumbbells, beanbags, clubs, wands, and an exercise machine called Dr. Schreber's Pangymnasticon. Lewis took much of his equipment from the *Turnvereins* (gymnastic or athletic clubs), which German immigrants had introduced to this country. Lewis believed in gymnastics for the jaw as well. He urged his students to chew a Graham cracker for six minutes.

Hydropathy, or the "water cure," was also popular for promoting health and beauty. Spas, built near natural mineral springs, catered to those who could afford them. A full daily treatment at one spa included being wrapped in wet sheets (to encourage sweating), a two-minute plunge bath in the springs, twenty to twenty-four glasses of water, two enemas, two sitz baths, and wet bandages around the neck, chest, and abdomen. A strict vegetarian diet was provided. Harriet Beecher Stowe was among those who praised the water cure. She claimed it showed "that the glow and joyousness of early life are things which may be restored."

The first half of the nineteenth century was a time of social reform. The abolitionist movement fought to end slavery. Feminists demanded equal rights for women—and realized that restrictive clothing was among the things holding women back (or down). By one estimate, a well-dressed woman might wear thirty-seven pounds of clothing during the winter, and more than half of this weight came in the form of petticoats. Feminists also noted the health problems caused by the corset.

In 1851, Amelia Jenks Bloomer, the deputy postmistress of Seneca Falls, New York, took the first step toward reforming

women's clothing. With her friends Elizabeth Cady Stanton and Libby Miller, she appeared in public wearing long, somewhat baggy pants. The "Bloomers," as they swiftly became known, were modeled after Turkish trousers that Libby Miller had seen in Europe. They also resembled the pantaloons that American female children had been wearing since about 1820.

The Bloomer outfit, which included a short skirt, set off a national frenzy of criticism. Elizabeth Cady Stanton's husband lost his bid for election to the New York State Senate because of his wife's connection to bloomers. And their son begged Elizabeth not to wear bloomers when she came to visit him at boarding school. (She didn't.)

However, some observers approved of the garment. A newspaper writer in San Francisco wrote in 1851: "The city was taken quite by surprise yesterday afternoon by observing a woman in company with her male companion . . . magnificently arrayed in a black satin skirt very short, with flowing red satin trousers, a splendid yellow crepe shawl, and a silk turban. . . . She really looked magnificent."

Bloomers never came into general use. However, a few women crossing the plains in wagon trains found that bloomers were practical for such journeys. In fact, Brigham Young, the leader of the Mormons, urged immigrants heading for the Mormon settlement in Utah to wear "desert costume," which included bloomers.

Keeping the fat off was important to the stylish man of the 1830s, 1840s, and 1850s. This illustration from Family Magazine *of 1834 advocates climbing, jumping, and running to keep trim. Women also practiced milder forms of exercise or calisthenics, such as swinging on bars.*

This sheet-music cover for "The New Costume Polka" celebrates the new style for women. The lithograph produced in 1851 is dedicated to Mrs. Lydia Bloomer - an error as her name was really Amelia. Nevertheless, the cover presents a positive view of a fashion that was often ridiculed.

Instead of dress reform, women got the hoop crinoline in 1856. This was a circular cage worn under a skirt or dress. It served the same function as the layers of heavy cloth petticoats, but weighed far less. Made of flexible steel, whalebone, or wicker, the crinoline was attached to the waist with cloth tapes. Amelia Bloomer announced her approval of it. Lighter and cooler in the summer, the crinoline became an immediate hit.

There were some drawbacks. The lightweight frame swayed with the motions of a woman's body, causing the hoop to tip up and provide a daring glimpse of ankles or legs. This was hot stuff

Dressing for the ball in 1858. The young woman needs help with the frame for her hoopskirt. Fashion decreed that women would be spared the weight of many petticoats, but they had to endure the cumbersome width of this kind of frame. It made going through doors and entering carriages difficult.

for the Victorian era. Words such as *pants* and *legs* were not even supposed to be spoken in mixed company. In some homes even piano legs were covered with lacy garments.

The worst thing about the crinoline was that its lightness enabled dresses to become even bigger. The style went to extremes, as women tried to have the largest possible dresses. Men could no longer kiss women who wore these hoop-widened skirts, because they couldn't get close enough. It was said that an average-size room would hold only three women wearing crinoline dresses. At dressmakers' shops, two employees had to stand on either side of the customer and lower the dress over her with poles.

Being in fashion meant displaying your finery. The "Sunday best" tradition was as old as the colonial settlements. Bertha Damon, who grew up in rural Connecticut, recalled, "In church everyone saw your clothes, that was where you wore your best. . . . We could sing out of hymnbooks looking right at the notes and tell whose ruffle was cut in the new way and how Abby Norton's sleeve was set."

Dressing up crossed all social lines. Even the enslaved Africans in the South put on a display on Sundays. Amos Lincoln, who had been a slave in Texas, recalled: "The gals dressed up on Sunday. All week they wear their hair all roll up with cotton. . . . Sunday come they comb the hair out fine. No grease on it. They want it naturally curly."

Immigrants from Germany and Ireland were coming to the United States in large numbers at this time. Many recalled that they put on their best clothing before landing. Others saved enough from the first money they earned to buy a new "American" outfit. Everybody wanted to dress right.

By mid-century, showing off new spring clothing at the Easter parade was a New York City custom. The great English novelist Charles Dickens commented on the women: "What rainbow silks and satins! What fluttering of ribbons and silk tassels, and displays of cloaks with gaudy hoods and linings!"

4

BEAUTY IN AN AGE OF EXCESS

 The Civil War from 1861 to 1865 was a wrenching experience for the United States. The conflict changed the nation forever. When it was over, however, a great era of expansion and wealth began. Railroads linked the country from ocean to ocean for the first time. Pioneers began to settle the vast area between the Mississippi River and California. Cities grew in size as immigrants came to America looking for economic opportunity. People made enormous fortunes from business, ranching, and railroad empires.

The beauty standards reflected this wealth. For the next twenty-five years, clothes became brighter and more gaudy. Lavish fabrics, heavier makeup, elaborate hairstyles, and expensive jewelry were all indications of the new style. The years after the Civil War are known as The Gilded Age for the splendid, and sometimes vulgar, display of wealth.

During this time, a new invention revolutionized the beauty business. In 1839 the Frenchman Louis Daguerre produced the earliest type of photograph. That was the beginning of the visual world we live in today. Within twenty years of Daguerre's first picture, photographs were being made cheaply and it became possible to make copies of them. Now people could see how a person really looked, without depending on a painter or engraver's version of them.

Advertisers discovered that pictures of beautiful women sold products. Other women could believe that if they used a certain

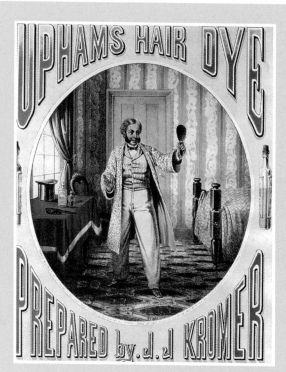

cream or remedy or hair product—then they too would become as beautiful as the woman in the photograph. Even after 140 years of evidence to the contrary, advertising is still based on that idea today.

These beautiful women became the fantasies for the beauty dreams of millions of others. The public loved to read about their private lives, even facts as trivial as what they ate at restaurants. People kept albums of photographs of famous actresses like Ada Isaacs Menken, Lotta Crabtree, Lillian Russell, and Lily Langtry. Langtry was one of the first to endorse a product—Pears' Soap. The Pears' company gave away free cards with her image and an advertising message. In exchange they paid Langtry 132 pounds (British money, but also her weight).

Photography (and good looks) became important to politics too. In 1860, Abraham Lincoln stopped by the New York photographic studio of Mathew Brady. Lincoln was starting his campaign for the presidency and was in New York to make a speech. Brady had photographed many famous people, but he had to use all his skill to make an acceptable picture of Lincoln. He urged Lincoln to pull his collar up. Lincoln understood. His thin, bony neck was too long.

The picture that resulted was reproduced thousands of times and sent all over the country. Today, we wouldn't think of it as a campaign photograph. Lincoln has no toothy grin, no confident eyes; he looks somber, and his hand rests on a book. Yet later, Lincoln declared that Brady's picture helped him win the election.

In the process of supplying uniforms for its army, the government took the measurements of millions of men, resulting in the first set of sizes for clothing. Also, before the Civil War, shoes did not come in right or left models. They were all "straights." For soldiers, however, the government ordered "crooked" shoes and boots, shaped for the left or the right foot. The soldiers found that they fit better, and demanded "crooked" shoes when they returned to civilian life.

War, raging across the nation, had a coarsening effect on society in general. Saloons and theaters entertained the troops with sexy shows—at least by the standards of the day. Prostitutes followed the armies as they marched. (The word *hooker*, meaning prostitute, comes from the women who catered to the troops commanded by General Joseph Hooker.)

After the war, the country was reunited. But—as with any war—some things never went back to the way they were before. A new era was beginning—one in which people flaunted wealth and sexuality more than before. The first new fashion for women reflected the changed temper of the times. It was the bustle. This consisted of a pad or wire frame under the dress at the rear. It was the New Look of the post-Civil War era. In effect (though nobody ever described it this way) it was a padded rear end.

Along with the bustle, women wore a tight corset and very high-heeled shoes that thrust the top part of the body forward. In many ways these corsets were the worst ever. They were extra long, reaching down to the hips and far up the back to keep the woman standing straight with breasts thrust forward.

Thin waists set off the large bosom and large rear. Since the hips and buttocks were extended backward, the total effect was an S-shaped silhouette called the Grecian bend. The ideal was to have large breasts on top of a corseted, flat stomach down to the hips, with the backside exaggerated by the bustle and a "half crinoline" that only protruded in the back.

The bustle and new look were the creations of Charles Worth, dressmaker for the empress Eugenie of France. Though Worth was born in England, he is regarded as the father of French *haute couture*—which means "high sewing," but has come to stand for the latest in high fashion. The new look definitely emphasized a fuller figure, or a *voluptuous* figure, as it was called. Marion Harland, an etiquette authority, wrote in 1880: "To be thin is no longer the acme [height] of feminine desires." Books such as *Plumpness: How to Achieve It* sold well. An English visitor noted that American women "are constantly having themselves weighed, and every ounce of increase is hailed with delight, and talked about with the most dreadful plainness of speech. When I asked a beautiful Connecticut girl how she liked the change, 'Oh! Immensely!' she said, 'I have gained eighteen pounds in flesh since last April.'"

Even the medical profession advised women that plump was healthy. Two neurologists wrote a book claiming that fat cells were critical to a well-balanced personality. People who lacked them (the unfortunate thin ones) tended to be overly nervous. And beauty adviser Harriet Hubbard Ayer noted, "A sweet temper and a bony woman never dwell under the same roof."

There were some body parts that were not improved by size—for instance the nose. Dr. Robert Tomes in his *Bazar Book of Decorum* advised: "The nose should never be fondled before company,

The super bustle was the first new fashion after the Civil War. Also called the Grecian bend, this style—worn here by a fashionable Fifth Avenue lady—was so exaggerated that women often had to kneel in carriages. (They couldn't sit.) After much ridicule, the fashion passed, but a smaller bustle remained in vogue for most of the rest of the century.

or, in fact, touched at any time, unless absolutely necessary. The nose, like other organs, augments [grows] in size by handling, so we recommend every person to keep his own fingers, as well as those of his friends or enemies, away from it."

Hairstyles grew more elaborate. Women supplemented their own hair with false hair attachments. These included wigs, braids, frizettes (forehead fringes), curls, waterfalls, and toupees. Julia Foraker recalled that when she was a student at Ohio Wesleyan University in 1873, the school tried to ban false hair because the students were neglecting their studies by spending too much time arranging their hair.

While hairstylists were predominantly male, women were the majority in another personal beauty business—manicuring. Manicure parlors began to appear in the 1870s. The new-style parlors had their origins in France. Monsieur Sitts, the foot doctor of King Louis Philippe, developed a system of improved hand care. Sitts used an orangewood stick adapted from a dental instrument to clean the nails and push back the cuticle after soaking the hand in soapy water.

THE START OF PLASTIC SURGERY

Surgeons in Sicily developed some plastic surgery techniques in the fifteenth century, but they were virtually forgotten until the nineteenth century. Dr. J. Mason Warren of Boston started to perform skin grafts in the 1840s. This kind of surgery was done on burn victims, but it led to plastic surgery for beauty purposes.

In 1887, John Orlando Roe performed cosmetic surgery to reduce the size and length of a patient's nose. He cut incisions within the nostrils and removed excess cartilage and bone. As an anesthetic, he injected cocaine under the skin inside the nose.

Five years later, Robert Fulton Weir of New York published *On Restoring Sunken Noses*, describing how he improved the appearance of a damaged nose. His method is still used today.

Sitts's niece took over his practice, and became the forerunner of the female manicurist. American beauty expert Harriet Hubbard Ayer visited Paris in the 1870s and came home to advocate the Sitts methods. Women found success as manicurists because other women thought letting a man hold their hand was too intimate.

Emancipation of the slaves created a larger market for beauty products intended for blacks. Unfortunately, most products at this time were aimed at helping blacks look more like whites. The four most popular black beauty products were Black Skin Remover, Black and White Ointment, Ozonized Ox Marrow, and Curl-I-Cure: a Cure for Curls.

Cosmetics of all kinds were back in style for the two decades after the Civil War. Those who embraced them eagerly were the wives of men made newly rich by wartime profits and the postwar railroad boom. They wanted to show off their wealth, and adopted such flashy styles as powdering their hair with gold and silver dust. When women appeared in mascara (for the first time) at the two fashionable resorts of Newport and Saratoga Springs, *Godey's Lady's Book* referred to these spas as "the Sodom and Gomorrah of our Union."

Some products introduced in the late nineteenth century have stood the test of time. In 1859, Robert A. Chesebrough noticed that oil-field workers used oil from oil rods to soothe bruises and cuts. He devised a petroleum jelly he called Vaseline and began selling it door-to-door. By 1870, Chesebrough had a major business, and his product was selling at the rate of a jar a minute.

In the 1870s, David McConnell was a book peddler. He gave away vials of perfume to his female customers. When he made the rounds again, he found that the perfume was more popular than the books. In 1886, McConnell created the Little Dot Perfume Set—five fragrances that he and his wife had brewed up themselves. Though the business was in New York, they called it the California Perfume Company. They hired a woman, Mrs. P. F. E. Albee, to sell the products door-to-door. The business they founded was renamed Avon Products in 1950, and Mrs. Albee has some 40 million successors ("Avon Ladies") around the world.

MADAME ROWLEY'S TOILET MASK

(OR FACE GLOVE).

The following are the claims made for Madame Rowley's Toilet Mask, and the grounds on which it is recommended to Ladies for Beautifying, Bleaching and Preserving the Complexion:

1st. The *Mask* is *Soft* and *Pliable* in form, and can be *Easily Applied* and *Worn* without *Discomfort* or *Inconvenience*.

2d. It is durable, and does not dissolve or come asunder, but holds its original shape.

3d. It has been *Analyzed* by *Eminent Scientists* and *Chemical Experts*, and pronounced *Perfectly Pure* and *Harmless*.

4th. With ordinary care the *Mask* will *Last for Years*, and its *valuable properties Never become Impaired*.

5th. The *Mask* is protected by letters patent, has been introduced ten years, and is the *nly Genuine* article of the kind.

6th. It is *Recommended* by *Eminent Physicians* and *Scientific Men* as a *substitute for injurious cosmetics*.

7th. The *Mask* is as *Unlike* the fraudulent appliances used for conveying cosmetics, etc., to the face *as day is to night*, and it bears no analogy to them.

8th. The *Mask* may be worn with *Perfect Privacy* if desired. The *Closest Scrutiny* cannot detect that it has been used.

The Toilet Mask (or Face Glove) in position to the face.
TO BE WORN THREE TIMES IN THE WEEK.

9th. It is a *Natural Beautifier* for *Bleaching* and *Preserving the Skin*, and *Removing Complexional Imperfections*

10th. The *Mask* is sold at a moderate price, *and one purchase ends the expense.*

11th. Hundreds of dollars uselessly expended for cosmetics, lotions and like preparations may be saved by those who possess it.

12th. *Ladies* in every section of the country are using the *Mask* with gratifying results.

13th. It is safe, simple, cleanly and effective for beautifying purposes, and never injures the most delicate skin.

14th. While it is intended that the *Mask* should be *Worn During Sleep*, it may be applied, *with equal good results*, at *Any Time*, to suit the convenience of the wearer.

15th. The *Mask* has received the testimony of well-known society and professional ladies who proclaim it to be the greatest discovery for beautifying purposes ever offered to womankind.

A Few Specimen Extracts from Testimonial Letters.

"I am so rejoiced at having found at last an article that will indeed improve the complexion."

"Every lady who desires a faultless complexion should provided with the Mask."

"My face is as soft and smooth as an infant's."

"I am perfectly delighted with it."

"As a medium for removing discolorations, softening and beautifying the skin, I consider it unequaled."

"It is, indeed, a perfect success—an inestimable treasure."

"I find that it removes freckles, tan, sunburn, and gives the complexion a soft, smooth surface."

"I have worn the mask but two weeks, and am amazed at the change it has made in my appearance."

"The Mask certainly acts upon the skin with a mild and beneficial result, making it smoother and clearer, and seeming to remove pimples, irritation, etc., with each application."

"For softening and beautifying the skin there is nothing to compare with it."

"Your invention cannot fail to supersede everything that is used for beautifying purposes."

"Those of my sex who desire to secure a pure complexion should have one."

"For bleaching the skin and removing imperfections I know of nothing so good."

"I have worn the Mask but three nights, and the blackheads have all disappeared."

"The Mask should be kept in every lady's toilet case."

"I must tell you how delighted I am with your Toilet Mask; it gives unbounded satisfaction."

"A lady was cured of freckles by eight nights' use of the Mask."

"The improvement in my complexion is truly marvelous."

"After three weeks' use of the Mask the wrinkles have almost disappeared."

"My sister used one for a spotted skin, and her complexion is now all that can be desired."

"It does even more than is claimed for it."

"I have been relieved of a muddy, greasy complexion after trying all kinds of cosmetics without success."

COMPLEXION BLEMISHES

may be hidden imperfectly by cosmetics and powders, but can only be removed permanently by the Toilet Mask. By its use every kind of spots, impurities, roughness, etc., vanish from the skin, leaving it soft, clear, brilliant and beautiful. It is harmless, costs little and saves its user money. It prevents and REMOVES

WRINKLES,

and is both a complexion preserver and beautifier. Famous society ladies, actresses, belles, etc., use it. VALUABLE ILLUSTRATED PAMPHLET, with proofs and full particulars, mailed free by

THE TOILET MASK COMPANY, 1164 Broadway, New York

A beautiful, unblemished, white complexion was a must for any budding beauty of the time. Creams and facial masks could help to achieve such a look. This ad for Madame Rowley's Toilet Mask or Face Glove also included testimonials from satisfied users.

In 1879 a worker made a mistake at the Procter and Gamble soap factory. He left the soap-making machine on too long. Air bubbles made the cakes of soap so light that they floated. That mistake led to what became possibly the most famous and longest-lasting advertising slogan. Harvey Proctor, one of the co-owners, thought up the name Ivory for the soap while he was at church listening to the reading of Psalms 45:8. The slogan "99 and 44/100 percent pure" has stuck to Ivory Soap ever since.

In the early 1880s, C. D. Fleet, a doctor from Virginia, came up with a formula for a balm to protect the lips. He had little success selling it and in 1912 sold the formula to American Home Products for five dollars. Today, Dr. Fleet's Chap Stick is used by young and old.

Like cosmetics, fashion in clothing was no longer an upper-class phenomenon. Women of all social classes adopted the new S-shaped look. One reason was the development of reusable patterns. The paper pattern, marked with different sizes, served as a template that could be placed on a piece of cloth to show where to cut the pieces of a garment. A woman only had to follow the directions, sew together the pieces she had cut out, and produce a new dress, suit, or other clothing.

Ellen Curtis Demorest first developed the sized pattern in 1858. She said she got the idea by watching her African American maid use brown paper to cut a pattern before making a dress. Five years later another pattern maker, Charles Butterick, got into the market. He was a tailor, and his wife suggested that making clothing would be easier if there were reusable patterns. Butterick too started with brown paper but later switched to tissue paper.

The Demorest and Butterick pattern businesses expanded rapidly. They were helped by the growing popularity of home sewing machines. By 1860, Americans had purchased over 100,000 sewing machines, enabling women throughout the country to make their own outfits. Demorest and Butterick competed in offering them the latest styles.

More department stores opened, imitating A. T. Stewart's. Marshall Field opened his store in Chicago in 1865. Another newcomer, R. H. Macy in New York, emphasized its stock of ready-to-wear clothing. By doing so, Macy's aimed at a less well-to-do customer than Stewart's. By the 1870s, New York's Fifth Avenue from Fourteenth to Twenty-third Streets was known as the "Ladies' Mile" because so many department stores were located there.

Two other retailers had multimillion dollar sales without any stores at all. Aaron Montgomery Ward left his job as a salesman at Marshall Field's in 1872 to start a mail-order business. He and a friend put out a one-page catalog, and found that people in rural areas, far from anything like a department store, were interested. Ward's advised its far-flung customers: "Give us your age and description of your general build, and in nine cases out of ten, we'll give you a fit." Repeat business showed that Ward's clothing department guessed people's sizes pretty well.

Richard Sears and Alvah Roebuck started selling watches by mail in 1886. By 1895 their catalog of all kinds of goods was 507 pages long, and many rural families sat around the fireplace at night looking at its pictures and dreaming what it would be like to have that, wear this.

Sears also took fashionable items and made them affordable. In 1868 a "croquet sandal" appeared at one of the nation's fancy resorts. It had a canvas upper attached to a rubber sole. By the end of the century it was known as the "sneaker," and Sears sold them for sixty cents a pair. Sears became the biggest retailer in the world by stressing both quality and price.

A host of new magazines appeared in the later nineteenth century. *Godey's Lady's Book* declined in popularity after the Civil War. In 1867 the first issue of *Harper's Bazar* (originally spelled that way) appeared. Three years later, the first issue of *McCall's* was published; at first it consisted only of patterns for clothes. In 1873, *Women's Home Companion*, in 1883 *Ladies' Home Journal*, and in 1885 *Good Housekeeping* all jumped into the growing field of women's magazines, and all thrived. The fact that the market would support so many shows how great the interest in fashion had become.

Elizabeth Custer, the wife of General George Armstrong Custer, described the importance of one such magazine to the women who followed their husbands to forts and towns on the remote prairie: "*Harper's Bazar* was as thoroughly read out there as at any point in its wide wanderings. . . . A charge of our brave men was made through the town hunting for black hair to re-model the antique coiffeurs of their better halves [that is, their wives]. It was no easy task, for the sun fades and streaks the glossiest lock out there, and the wind breaks and dries the silkiest mane."

Ladies' Home Journal introduced something new to women's magazines. Cyrus Curtis, the publisher, accepted advertising. Before then, magazines made money solely from the price paid by readers. From this point on, advertisers would become more and more important to a magazine's income. That of course meant that the publication had to please both its readers and its advertisers.

The post-Civil War man adopted a new style. He wanted to be bigger and brawnier than the small-featured men of the early nineteenth century. His models were men like Buffalo Bill Cody, the western hero and showman; Diamond Jim Brady, the railroad tycoon known for his gargantuan appetite; and John L. Sullivan, the boxer who boasted he "could lick any man in the world." All three of these men had one thing in common: They were big, and big was the thing to be.

Though the nineteenth century had no men's fashion magazines, men still wanted to look good. New York City tailors displayed fashion plates from London in their shop windows. Demorest and Butterick offered patterns for men's suits, copied from the New York tailors.

Young men started to wear high-buttoned jackets and matching pants. This was a novel idea; previously the coat and the pants seldom came in the same cloth. Many men still sported checked pants with a plain cloth coat. In 1886 tobacco heir Griswold Lorillard wore a black smoking jacket, rather than a formal coat with tails, to a party at the Tuxedo Country Club. Though a newspaper reported that Lorillard looked like "a royal footman," the style caught on. Today Lorillard's fashionable suit is called a tuxedo, after the town in New York State where it first appeared.

Mathew Brady's campaign photograph of Lincoln showed him clean shaven. But by the time Lincoln was inaugurated, he had grown a beard. During the campaign he received a letter from Grace Bedell, an eleven-year-old girl. She had seen him giving a speech and suggested that he would look better with whiskers. When he traveled to Washington as the president-elect, he stopped in upstate New York to tell Grace, "You see, I have let these whiskers grow for you." He was the first president to have a beard. Five out of the next six presidents did, however, as the fashion caught on among American men.

There were many popular styles of both mustaches and beards. Some beards became a badge of various professions: a rectangular beard marked an engineer; a pointed (or Vandyke) beard signified an artist (or would-be artist); a bushy beard was appropriate for a naval officer. In the 1840s, while a student at West Point, Ambrose F. Burnside grew bushy side whiskers. When he became a general in the Civil War, many imitated the style, calling it *sideburns*, in his honor.

Barbershops became social gathering places for males during this time. "Man talk," including some dirty jokes, could go on here without worry about giving offense to females. Almost every shop had a copy of the *Police Gazette*, which was the *Playboy* of the day. Irish immigrant Richard K. Fox, the publisher, built a large circulation with a combination of sex, crime, and sports. The beautiful women depicted in the *Gazette* were all of the stout, fleshy variety.

Women across the country imitated famous beauties of the theater world—to a degree. Few women were as daring as Ada Isaacs Menken who appeared on stage riding a horse while wearing flesh-colored tights that made her appear nude. But many women bought Pears' Soap because the actress Lily Langtry endorsed it. Langtry, born in the British island of Jersey, was dubbed "the Jersey Lily." She introduced the jersey, or form-fitting sweater, to American fashion.

Lillian Russell, star of New York's musical stage, fit the model of a voluptuous beauty—in part because she often ate dinner with her massive friend Diamond Jim Brady. Russell became known as "The American Beauty," and a deep red rose, still popular, was given that name in her honor.

 Lillian Russell was one of the great beauties of the last half of the nineteenth century. She started as a musical comedy star as a young woman, and kept her popularity even as her size dramatically increased.

56

Then as now, women—especially the young—tried to match the standard they saw in pictures of such famous beauties. Young women were told that success for them lay in finding a husband, and personal beauty was their most important asset. The novelist Caroline Lee Hentz wrote (of a character named after herself): "It never entered into the heart of Caroline that men could be enslaved by any other charm but beauty. From [childhood] every instruction she had received seemed to [encourage] external attraction. She was excluded from the sun and air. . . . Her hands were imprisoned in gloves. . . . She was not permitted to read or study by candlelight, lest she should dim the starry brightness of her eyes, or to take long walks, lest her feet should be enlarged by too much exercise. 'Katy, my love, don't eat too much, it will make your complexion coarse.' "

THE GIBSON GIRL
TO THE CHRISTY GIRL

The years between 1890 and 1919 were pivotal ones for the American beauty business. Women took the first steps toward freeing themselves from restrictive garments. The number of women working outside the home tripled in the last third of the nineteenth century. Inventions such as the typewriter and telephone created new jobs for women as typists and telephone operators (at first called "hello girls"). Women also found work as teachers, nurses, stenographers, and department store clerks. These women needed clothes that were practical in the workplace, but they still wanted them to be fashionable. The "power suit" of this time was the shirtwaist and skirt.

The women's rights movement flourished as well. One of its chief goals was women's suffrage, or the right to vote. In 1912, when a huge New York suffragette rally marched down Fifth Avenue, the leaders of the demonstration were proudly wearing makeup. They associated the right to enhance their looks with equality.

Indeed, as the twentieth century dawned, some saw beauty as "the natural right" of every woman. Optimists believed that beauty would be available for all. Some predicted that science would conquer aging and find ways to increase anyone's personal beauty. Others thought that the human race would become increasingly beautiful because both men and women would choose beautiful mates, and thus have more beautiful children. No one discussed what would happen to those less favored by the gods of beauty.

The beauty ideal was the Gibson girl. Tall, with a narrow waist, she still was endowed with a large bosom and hips. Her face was immediately recognizable, with its high forehead, Cupid's-bow mouth, and small, straight nose. Thick, glossy, dark hair, swept up in a large pompadour, covered her head. She wore a shirtwaist with a long skirt encircled by a belt that emphasized her small waist.

The Gibson girl was the creation of artist Charles Dana Gibson, and first appeared in 1890. She took the nation by storm. Lithographs and woodcuts, dishes, spoons, and even wallpaper carried her image. Clothing and dances were named for her, and pictures of women who looked like her appeared in magazines and newspapers. Gibson found that he could sell original drawings of her for one thousand dollars each; that was more than the annual income of an average American.

The appeal of the Gibson girl sprang from the fact that she was tied to so many parts of American society. Feminists approved the Gibson girl as a model of the "new woman." Dress reformers endorsed her clothes. However, corset makers liked the look too, because the waist was still so tight that corsets could not be abandoned. The fact that the Gibson girl was often shown golfing or bicycling won the approval of physical fitness fans. She was shown at horse shows, balls, and the opera and thus seemed representative of high society. But working women identified with her because of the practical clothing she wore.

The shirtwaist that the Gibson girl wore was modeled after a man's dress shirt, although it buttoned in the back. An American design, it was a sign of independence from French fashions. Shirtwaists could cost as little as $1.50 or, with trimmings such as ruffles and embroidery, up to hundreds of dollars. It came with either straight sleeves or puffy ones called "leg of mutton."

Natalie Dana, then a young woman, recalled, "Our waists were laced in, our collars high, and our skirts swept the ground. Long steel pins and tight veils kept our large hats in place. Though we held up our skirts in correct folds with our right hands and tried to keep them from touching the streets, my legs were always black to the knee when I dressed for dinner."

The Gibson girl had lots of hair, and the rest of America's women followed her lead. Her pompadour was puffed up by being rolled over a horsehair "rat" or pad. Professional hairstylists could put together this complicated style best. So hair salons mushroomed all over.

There was a Gibson man too. He had a square, smooth-shaven jaw and hair that was slicked down and parted in the middle. The man very much resembled Charles Gibson's close friend Richard Harding Davis, a journalist renowned for his courage and style. Though Davis was barrel-chested, he probably wore a corset of his own, for pictures show him with a slim waist—like the Gibson man.

Though men now sported clean-shaven chins, mustaches remained in vogue for a few more years. The barber's straight razor, sharpened on a leather strop each time it was used, could be tricky to use at home. In 1903 a man named King Camp Gillette offered his new "safety razor" that used disposable blades. The next year, he sold 90,000 razors and 12 million blades. He became rich by inventing one of the first products that customers would use and throw away.

Slimness was back in fashion. Thomas B. Reed, the Speaker of the House of Representatives, declared, "No gentleman ever weighs more than two hundred pounds." Actually, William Howard Taft, president of the United States from 1909 to 1913, weighed more than *three* hundred pounds. But as the heaviest president in the nation's history, he endured the ridicule of cartoonists. One time, he got stuck in the White House bathtub.

Physical fitness was in vogue. At the Chicago Columbian Exposition in 1893, showman Florenz Ziegfeld exhibited the "Hungarian strongman," Eugene Sandow. Photographs of the muscular Sandow sold well. Inspired by them, a young man named Bernarr Macfadden began a fitness crusade. Macfadden opened a "temple of body worship" in Chicago, where he promoted nutrition and "kinesitherapy," or weight lifting. Macfadden wrote books and published magazines devoted to health and fitness. His first editorial for his magazine *Physical Culture* summed up his philosophy: "Weakness is a crime; don't be a criminal."

The barbershop was a popular male hangout in the early years of the new century. Since being clean shaven was fashionable—although mustaches were still allowed—the barber was the main beauty consultant for males. Customers could pick up community news there as well. This photograph shows Rudy Sohn's Kansas barbershop in 1903.

Macfadden was typical of the times in stressing self-improvement. Women had always *wanted* to be beautiful, but now people were telling them they *should* be. Beauty specialist Harriet Hubbard Ayers advised working women that their appearance was key to their success. Annette Kellermann, a champion swimmer, wrote a beauty manual that told women how important good looks were in attracting a husband.

Cosmetic surgery was in its infancy. Surgeons tried to reshape noses, pin back ears, and give face-lifts. Sometimes a beautician would use electricity or acid to remove the top layer of skin. Paraffin was inserted under the skin to make cheeks rounder or firm up sagging eyelids.

Such methods were beyond the means of the average person. One thing that everyone could do, however, was exercise. The biggest fad of the 1890s was bicycling. When women started to pedal, they threw aside the notion of female fragility. Women sat astride the bicycle (whereas they still sat sidesaddle when riding horses). Thus, skirts that split, culottes, or knickerbockers were necessary for women cyclists.

THE GIBSON GIRL'S HAT

Large and elaborate hats went with the Gibson girl hairstyle. Long feathers were prized as trimming for the new hat styles. In fact, sometimes women's hats sported whole stuffed birds. A favorite was the bird of paradise; a hat with one of these could cost more than one hundred dollars. Eventually, laws were passed forbidding the use of certain kinds of feathers in order to save the birds from extinction.

Hat pins, to hold these large and heavy hats in place, reached their largest size at this time. Sometimes they were so long that people standing or walking near a woman complained about being stuck with a protruding pin. Legislatures in both Louisiana and New Jersey outlawed hat pins over a certain size.

Genteel women played croquet or golf. Some went boating. Those looking for something more energetic took up tennis. Long skirts made running around a tennis court difficult, so a few daring women wore bloomers. Ava Willian Astor, who had married one of the nation's richest men, shocked Newport society in 1893 by wearing bloomers in public. Women's colleges started to provide physical education and sports, and bloomers gained acceptance in the gym.

In the 1890s female swimmers wore virtually everything a woman would wear in public—including a corset. Modesty did not stop there. A woman had to enter a contraption called a bathing machine, which resembled a small hut on wheels. As she changed from her everyday clothes into her swimming outfit, the bathing machine was rolled into the water. There, the woman could emerge

The Gibson look and women's shirtwaists were used for leisure and sporting activities as well as business. Bicycling was the great fad and outdoor activity of the turn of the century. These two couples are enjoying a fine day in Denver, Colorado.

63

Bathing beauties of the turn of century. These five girls posed at Coney Island beach in their swimsuits. Actually the suits were quite daring for the time. Some women still wore bathing dresses that reached their ankles.

from a door facing away from the shore and walk down steps into the water. Even so, the sight of her was protected from men's eyes by an awning called a "modesty hood." (She couldn't get far from the bathing machine, because when the swimsuit got wet it became heavy enough to sink most wearers.) When Annette Kellerman, the Australian swimmer, appeared in a sleeveless one-piece suit that ended at the knees, in 1907, police in Atlantic City, New Jersey, immediately arrested her.

Men started to wear swimsuits at this same time. The male swimsuit was considerably briefer than the ones for women, but it still included a tank top that covered the chest but not the arms.

Women also did calisthenics (of a sort) to slim down. The actress Lillian Russell decided to reduce after being called an elephant by a critic in 1896. The New York *World* reported that she rolled over on the floor 250 times every morning. Russell claimed this was a beauty secret in Turkish harems.

Massaging was another popular technique to get rid of fat. Reducing salons opened for the first time, and many of them used massaging machines. The Gardner Reducing Machine, for example, enveloped the body between rows of adjustable rollers. Dr. Kellogg's sanatorium in Battle Creek, Michigan, had vibrating chairs and platforms, trunk rollers, chest beaters, and stomach beaters.

Electricity, being modern and thus better (according to the ads), was used for massaging too. One invention was a chair with electrodes fixed to the seat and back. The patient settled into the chair and was swathed with wet towels before the electricity was turned on. Though this sounds like a sure way to electrocute yourself, a session in the chair was advertised as equal to a ten-mile run.

One way or another, fat now needed to be fought. Dr. Emma E. Walker wrote in the *Ladies Home Journal* in 1905: "It is better to be too thin than too plump, for an excess of fat may cause serious mischief. It makes one heavy and awkward, and finally the 'fat walk'—the waddling gait you know so well—develops, and I beg you to avoid this!"

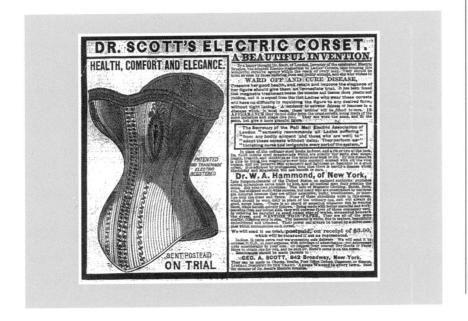

To get the small waist that was popular at the time, a strong corset was needed. Indeed, the corset was the most important undergarment of the nineteenth century. In the 1890s, when electrical products were brand new, George A. Scott of New York advertised an electrical corset that he claimed could even cure disease.

Magazines and books recommended many diets and "eating cures." One, popularized by the Englishman William Banting, was so well known that many people called dieting "banting." Banting's book advised eating lean meats, dry toast, soft-boiled eggs, and green vegetables.

Dr. Kellogg, searching for the perfect diet and health food, came up with granola in 1877. By the 1890s—sweetened, enriched, and prepared in a new cooking process—it became Kellogg's Corn Flakes.

Fasting was, of course, the ultimate diet and it too became a fad. People fasted for political as well as beauty reasons. "Hunger artists" staged public fasts to promote a variety of social causes, including women's suffrage. It was during this era that the condition called *anorexia* was first identified. Often written about today, anorexia is the abnormal fear of being fat, to the point where a person starves because of an incorrect self-image. Jennie Hill of Akron, Ohio, died in 1885 after fasting twenty-five days, eating only small bites of oranges and water. She was only fifteen.

The dawn of a new century marked the beginning of fresh styles and a more permissive era. In the first two decades, young, unmarried women and men flocked to urban dance halls, amusement parks, and the movies. Ragtime music set the rhythm for a century that would see a faster pace and greater freedom in American lifestyles.

Women wanted clothes that let them move more easily. Skirts started to move upward. Henry Collins Brown described "the sensation caused by the young lady who first trod the streets of New York in a skirt…that was actually three inches from the ground. Crowds followed her, shrieking with loud and derisive laughter." By 1916 skirts had almost reached the knee, but then they fell again. It would take another ten years for them to reach that height again.

Several influential trendsetters created a new "look" that replaced the Gibson girl. Paul Poiret, a French designer, attracted attention by de-emphasizing the waistline. Poiret's designs emphasized a more slender, small-breasted, slim-hipped, and long-legged look. Poiret did not like the way corsets raised and emphasized the bustline. He declared, "From now on, breasts will no longer be worn!"

Though it was a relief for women to discard the corset, they were hampered in a new way by another Poiret design. He introduced a straight skirt that was so tight that underneath it women had to wear a *hobble garter* attached to the upper part of their calves. This garter had one end attached to each leg; its purpose was to keep women from taking long strides when they walked. In this hobble skirt, women minced along, taking tiny steps. It was almost impossible to climb stairs while wearing one.

The pompadour hairstyle didn't suit the new style of clothes. A process called *marcelling* arrived from France just before World War I. It had been invented by Marcel Gateau, who started as a stable boy currying horses' tails. Marcelling required a curling iron to heat and shape the hair.

The Swiss-born hairdresser Charles Nessler invented the first permanent waving system in 1904. His method at first involved winding the hair spirally, using borax pads and a gas heater. Getting a permanent wave took six to ten hours. After World War I, however, an electric waving machine made the permanent wave more popular.

Irene Castle was another important trendsetter. She and her husband and dance partner, Vernon, introduced many dance crazes—the bunny hug, turkey trot, and tango among them. The Castles were images of grace and elegance, and they made dancing look like fun. Irene was slender and popularized a new, boyish look for women. She bobbed, or cut short, her hair and wore a headband of seed pearls on her forehead. Her style was the forerunner of the flapper fashions that would later characterize the 1920s. (Vernon's contribution to men's styles was the popularization of the wristwatch.)

The other great influence on styles after 1910 was the movies. Mary Pickford was the first female superstar. She had small features, a clear complexion, bow-shaped lips, sad eyes, and blond curls. Audiences found her the very model of purity and innocence.

Pickford began her career when she was sixteen and continued to play childlike roles until she was thirty-two. Audiences knew she was married to husky, muscular movie hero Douglas Fairbanks, but they insisted on seeing their favorite actress looking like a young teenager.

Opposed to the heroine was the vamp—sexual, sophisticated, and urbane. The first of this type was Theda Bara, whose career lasted only from 1914 to 1918 but left a long legacy. Press agents spread the story that the actress had exotic origins in Egypt. (Her last name was Arab spelled backward. In real life she was Theodosia Goodman from Ohio.) Theda Bara wore highly exaggerated eye makeup created for her by Helena Rubinstein. She maintained her exotic aura by agreeing to be interviewed only in rooms lined with black velvet, with burning incense scenting the air. She was the first Hollywood sex symbol.

The popularity of movie and stage stars brought makeup back into respectable status. Around 1900 women started to openly wear makeup. The Sears catalog—always a good gauge of public acceptance—advertised rouge sticks, powder puffs, and, a little later, lip gloss and eye shadow. The first liquid nail polish appeared in 1907, as did the first synthetic hair color. (Earlier hair dyes had been based on vegetables or fruits.)

The most important change in the beauty business at the beginning of the twentieth century was that it became a big business. As more and more women found jobs, they had more money to spend. Advertisers sought to get them to spend it on beauty products. And the beauty business offered unique opportunities for women to start their own enterprises. Women were opening salons and beauty schools, writing books and giving courses on achieving beauty.

Three very determined women made their names household words. The first was Elizabeth Arden, born Florence Nightingale Graham in a small village in Ontario, Canada, in 1878. When she went to nursing school, she saw the possibilities for a beauty cream. Though she herself had a beautiful complexion, Florence noticed other women with scarred or blemished skin. They needed a product at a time when "nice women" didn't wear makeup.

When she was thirty, Florence came to New York and found a job with a "beauty culturist." This shop used massage and creams to rejuvenate skin. In 1910 she opened her first salon in a location on fashionable Fifth Avenue. There, she developed her own beauty products. It was at this time that she took the name Elizabeth Arden.

She was determined to make her salon look luxurious. All the rooms were pink, which became her signature color. Customers came for facial treatments and manicures, but Arden suggested makeup for special events such as a dance or party. She was skilled at putting on tinted powder and other kinds of makeup so that it wasn't obvious. The Arden touch typically stressed elegance and subtlety.

Arden realized that people who couldn't afford her salon might still buy her products. She persuaded Stern's, a department store on Forty-second Street, to stock some samples. They sold out immediately, and the Elizabeth Arden empire was launched. Today, the company she founded has beauty salons around the world.

Arden visited Paris in 1914, and may have stopped at the salon owned by the woman who would become her biggest competitor—Helena Rubinstein. Born in Poland around 1871, Rubinstein later said that her mother was the inspiration for her success. "Women influence the world through love," Rubinstein recalled her mother saying. Rubinstein herself added that it was her mother "who gave me the sense of confidence and self-fulfillment which can come of taking regular care of one's physical assets."

When she was about twenty, Rubinstein went to Australia, where an uncle lived. She brought along twelve jars of a beauty cream produced in Poland. She opened her first beauty salon in Melbourne in 1902. A few years later, she started one in London. There, she increased her knowledge of makeup by discussing it with actresses, the only people besides prostitutes who regularly wore cosmetics at that time. In fact, when her "respectable" customers came to her salon, they arrived in closed carriages so that no one would see them.

It was on to Paris in 1910. By now she was offering Swedish massage to her customers, one of whom was the French author

Colette. When World War I broke out in 1914, Rubinstein went to the United States.

"The first thing I noticed," she later recalled, "was the whiteness of the women's faces and the oddly grayish color of their lips. Only their noses, mauve with cold, seemed to stand out. . . . So I said to myself, here is not only a new country but a huge new market for my products."

Her optimism was justified. She opened a salon seven blocks north of Elizabeth Arden's. (Arden responded by increasing the size of her salon.) Before long, Rubinstein had expanded to San Francisco, Philadelphia, New Orleans, Atlantic City, and Chicago. Rubinstein's salons were more dramatic in their decor than Arden's. Typically, a Rubinstein room had dark blue velvet walls and red baseboards, and was decorated with sculptures. She insisted that any woman could be beautiful, once remarking, "There are no ugly women, only lazy ones."

Even more successful in her own way was Madam C. J. Walker, the first American woman to make herself a millionaire. She started life as Sarah Breedlove. Her parents were ex-slaves, and Sarah worked as a laundress when she was very young. But she had big ideas. In 1905 she invented a comb that straightened hair without damaging it, as earlier products had done. She also developed a hair pomade for black women.

By 1910, Sarah was selling these products door-to-door in Indianapolis. She found that black women were eager to buy her products, and before long she trained a sales force of young black women. Madam Walker had a three-point program for her employees: (1) becoming economically self-sufficient; (2) divine inspiration; (3) the importance of health and beauty. Her magazine, *The Woman's Voice*, spotlighted Walker products, gave beauty advice, and featured the work of talented African American women writers.

Madam Walker employed over 10,000 women by the time of her death in 1919. She had accomplished in nine years what most people could not do in a lifetime. She left instructions in her will that only a woman was to head her company.

When the United States entered World War I in 1917, it ended an era in women's fashion. The War Industries Board, created to organize the war effort at home, asked women not to wear corsets. The reason? The stays in the garments were often made of steel needed for the war effort. Women began to wear the slimming undergarments called girdles.

During the war the all-day dress emerged as the standard outfit for women. It was tailored in style and simple enough to be mass-produced. The dress was made of silk because wool was needed for military uniforms. The silk dress remained a favorite after the war as well.

The scientist Ernest Mahler developed a cotton substitute made of wood—called cellulose—for use as a bandage. Red Cross nurses found another use for cellulose as a sanitary napkin. In 1921, Kimberly-Clark began to market the product as Kotex. (Previously women had used absorbent cloths that they washed and reused.)

Men who weren't in the armed forces still liked to don civilian versions of military wear. German fighter pilots, including such dashing figures as Baron von Richtofen, cut the tails off their long leather coats to fit into the cockpits of their planes. This "bomber jacket" became a favorite of men in countries on both sides of the war. Similarly, the British coatmaker Thomas Burberry created a waterproof cotton coat with such details as storm flaps, epaulets, and metal rings to carry grenades. This trench coat has been a perennial favorite in men's styles ever since.

Finally, another idealized American female emerged from the war. Howard Chandler Christy, a magazine illustrator, was assigned to create a recruiting poster. He borrowed heavily from both Irene Castle and Mary Pickford when he created a young woman saying, "Gee I wish I were a man! I'd join the Navy."

The "Christy girl" actually resembled a boy with her short hair, flat chest, and narrow hips. She would prove to be the model for the next decade, in which American women were liberated as never before.

Life

FEBRUARY 18, 1926   Teaching old Dogs new tricks   PRICE 15 CENTS

6

THE FLAPPER

The "Roaring Twenties" were a time when the country seemed to be having one long party. The stock market soared to new heights. The Eighteenth Amendment to the Constitution, ratified in 1919, outlawed alcoholic drinks, but nobody seemed to pay any attention. The fact that alcohol was illegal only seemed to make it more desirable.

On August 18, 1920, the Nineteenth Amendment to the Constitution was ratified, giving women the right to vote. Women seized the opportunity to liberate themselves in virtually every other way as well. They smoked cigarettes, painted their faces, drank cocktails, and wore dresses that showed their legs (from the knees down, anyway).

The twenties were a time when young people flouted old-fashioned values. They discarded what remained of nineteenth-century style and fashion. Even the slang of the 1920s sounded new and irreverent. A good-looking woman was called a beaut, the cat's pajamas, the cat's whiskers, and the cat's meow. Her male counterpart was known as a lounge lizard, jelly bean, cake-eater, or jazzbo.

The most famous name for the new woman of the twenties was the flapper. The term described a fad in which young women wore rubber galoshes—unfastened, so that they flapped when they walked. The galoshes fad didn't last long, but the name stuck.

The flapper herself gloried in a boyish figure with a flat chest and no hips. She had a young baby face with wide-open eyes, tiny lips, and rosy cheeks. She had no waistline. Most importantly,

Facing page: This February 1926 cover of Life shows a drawing by John Held, Jr., who popularized the flapper look. No corset created the woman's shape, and for the first time she was allowed to show off her legs. The girl is dancing the popular Charleston.

legs—for so long invisible—would become a major beauty element. Flappers displayed their legs to good effect while doing such vigorous dances as the Charleston and the Black Bottom. Dance parties were so popular that people started having them in the afternoons ("tea dances") as well as the evenings.

John Held, a magazine illustrator, drew the classic flapper as a cartoon character for *Life* magazine (a humor magazine at that time). He dubbed her Margy the boop-boop-a-doop girl. She wore high heels that supported impossibly skinny legs and always carried a thin black cigarette holder. A long string of pearls was usually flying around her neck as she danced.

In John Held's drawings, Margy's date was "Joe College." He wore wide-legged pants and a letter sweater or a blazer. When the weather turned cold (and sometimes even if it didn't), Joe College donned a full-length raccoon coat. The look wasn't complete without a ukulele to serenade his flapper girlfriend.

A new item of clothing made its appearance: the brassiere. Formerly, women wore a chemise next to their skin, and the corset shaped the breasts. One day in 1914, Polly Jacob, a young New Yorker whose parents were in the Social Register, decided to do something about restrictive underwear. As a teenager, she wrote later, she had been encased "in a sort of boxlike armor of whalebone and pink cordage [that] ran upwards from the knee to under the armpit."

Polly sewed two handkerchiefs and a pink ribbon together to make the first brassiere. She patented the idea and tried to sell bras to New York stores. Outside of Polly's friends, however, few people seemed to want one. In the end, Polly sold the patent to Warner Brother's Corset Company for $1,500. It was the greatest bargain that company ever made.

Warner had some competition from another brassiere created by Ida Cohen Rosenthal. A Russian Jewish immigrant, Rosenthal developed a more structured bra in the early 1920s. Her version added tucks in the material to make cups, as well as having snaps in the back for firmer support. In 1923, Rosenthal and her husband started the Maiden Form brassiere company.

During the twenties, women showed more of their bodies than ever before. That created a need for new kinds of accessories and personal grooming. For the first time, women shaved their legs and under their arms. In 1920, Odorono, the first commercial deodorant, came onto the market.

Previously, women's stockings were usually made of plain cotton or wool. Now that legs had emerged from their hiding places under dresses and petticoats, women began to wear fancy embroidered stockings. Cotton hosiery tended to bag at the knee, however, and women discovered silk stockings. The most popular were flesh colored to make the legs look bare. The first silk stockings had seams running up the back, and a new grooming habit for women was checking to see if the seams were straight.

The big decision for a girl wanting to be a flapper was "bobbing" her hair. Short hair was a break with the tradition that a woman's "crowning glory" was long hair. The experience was such

THE KING TUT CRAZE

Fads of all kinds swept the country in the 1920s. One of the biggest began in 1922 when British archaeologists unearthed the tomb of Egyptian King Tutankhamen. The news set off a "King Tut" craze that inspired many new fashions and beauty products. Women wore clothing in so-called Egyptian colors—Coptic and lotus blue, Saqqara and mummy brown, and cornelian. Jewelry manufacturers sold pins and rings resembling scarab beetles and lotus blossoms—supposedly modeled after jewelry in Tut's tomb.

Women outlined their eyes with kohl and rinsed their hair with henna to make it darker. Palmolive Soap advertisements claimed that the product was made from the same oils that Cleopatra had used. Fashion designers used many Egyptian motifs in their clothing, including a King Tut swimming cap and the "mummy wrap," a dress that fit nearly as close as a mummy's bandages.

a big step that beauty salons provided smelling salts for customers to use while their hair was being bobbed.

And the reaction to women who bobbed their hair was often ferocious. Ministers preached sermons against the style. In Missouri a child testified against her own mother in a custody hearing, saying, "We don't believe mother is a Christian woman. She bobs her hair." Stores fired women employees for cutting their hair. Doctors claimed the practice would ultimately cause baldness.

Yet short hair went with automobiles, movies, short skirts, jazz, cigarette smoking, and defying the Prohibition law. Best of all, it made women feel liberated. Mary Garden, an opera singer, bobbed her hair in 1927 when she was fifty. She explained why: "Bobbed hair is a state of mind, and not merely a new manner of dressing my head. . . . I consider getting rid of our long hair one of the many little shackles that women have cast aside in their passage to freedom." Many women believed that they could not be chic without a bob.

As the style caught on, women rushed to beauty parlors to have their hair bobbed. The number of hair-cutting salons rose from 5,000 to 23,000 in the decade. Some women broke with another tradition: They went to the men's barbershop, because the flapper cut wasn't much longer than a man's. The short hairstyle was a boon to hair professionals because it required frequent trimming.

Another short style was the "curly bob" with tight "spit curls" next to the scalp. To keep these curls in place, women used a new invention, the bobby pin, which got its name from the bobbed hairstyle. Women who didn't have naturally curly hair used sticky lotions, hot irons to "marcel" their hair, or permanent waves. The permanent-wave process had gone electric—although the machines looked like something out of a mad scientist movie. Many women started going to a hairdresser once a week for a set and comb out.

The cosmetics industry ballooned during the twenties. Like short hair and a short skirt, makeup represented emancipation and modernity. The flapper flaunted her painted face and made no effort to gain a "natural" look. She applied cosmetics in public—

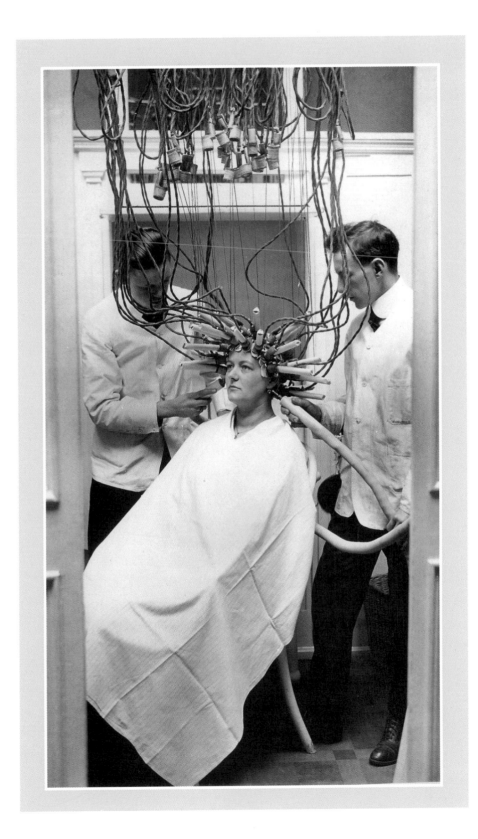

The permanent became a popular way of curling one's hair in the early decades of the twentieth century. At that time, the machinery was only available at the beauty parlor. All those wires stayed on the woman's head for hours.

breaking a strong taboo of the past. Her favorite shade of lipstick was bright red, which made lips look "ready for a kiss." She also used rouge heavily on her face, her knees, and even her earlobes.

Black kohl-rimmed eyes matched the flapper's scarlet lips. Women outlined their eyes to make them look larger and rounder. (At first they used burned matchsticks, but eyeliners soon appeared.) Mascara started to show up on the lashes. In 1915, T. L. Williams saw his sister Mabel using petroleum jelly on her eyelashes, and he marketed the idea as Mabelline. In 1920, Nina Sussman mixed a batch of mascara in her Paris kitchen and started her company, Aziza. Three years later, a new tool appeared for curling eyelashes—the Kurlash. Women also plucked their eyebrows and used eyebrow pencil to get the brow line they wanted.

The French cosmetic firm Coty brought out air-spun powder in a box designed by Leon Bakst, an artist who designed sets for the famous Ballet Russe. Women began to carry compacts with powder and a powder puff everywhere they went. Purses and handbags were made with a spare compartment for the compact.

People still believed that fat was unhealthy. Makers of cigarettes and chewing gum promoted the idea that their products could help you lose weight. Such products as Silph Chewing Gum, Slends Fat Reducing Chewing Gum, or Elfin Fat Reducing Gum Drops promised to take off the pounds. Advertisements for Lucky Strike cigarettes showed boyish-looking aviator Amelia Earhart and other celebrities advising, "Reach for a Lucky instead of a sweet."

Men had their own ideal—one of strength and muscularity. In 1922 one of the magazines published by fitness guru Bernarr Macfadden ran a contest for "the world's most perfectly developed man." The winner was Angelo Siciliano, who won again the next year. He had come to America with his parents when he was eleven.

Siciliano's story was an inspiring one. He had been a skinny teenager, and recalled that bullies had kicked sand in his face at the Coney Island beach. He looked around for something that would help him develop muscles, and found his inspiration by watching lions in the Prospect Park Zoo. As they stretched, he noticed, they pitted their muscles against each other. He began to work out at the YMCA, using that principle, which he later called "dynamic tension."

After winning Macfadden's contest, Siciliano changed his name to Charles Atlas. He began to sell a pamphlet explaining dynamic tension. Advertisements in magazines depicted in cartoon form the now-famous story of the bully on the beach, tormenting the "90-pound weakling." Generations of boys in the United States would try the Charles Atlas method.

Movies were more popular than ever, and Hollywood stars set beauty standards for the rest of the country. The sexiest female star of the 1920s was said to be Clara Bow. She became known as the "It girl" after she starred in a movie titled simply *It*. Women tried to copy the It girl's kohl-rimmed eyes and Cupid's-bow lips. Thousands asked hairdressers to give them Bow's cheek curls.

Bow had fulfilled the dream of many young women: She had gotten a role in a movie by winning a beauty contest sponsored by *Photoplay* magazine. Her screen persona was classic flapper—self-assured and impudent. She flaunted her sexuality. The line between screen fantasy and reality seemed blurred in her case. Magazines reported on her scandalous private life. She smoked, drank, and danced till dawn. Late in the decade, the arrival of talking movies killed her career, for she had a thick Brooklyn accent that didn't match the fantasy her looks created.

The male star of the decade was Rudolph Valentino. His Latin looks with quivering nostrils and flaming eyes literally made women faint in the movie theaters. Valentino came to this country from Italy in 1913. He worked as a gardener, dancer, gigolo, and movie extra. In 1920 he got his big break playing a tango dancer in *The Four Horsemen of the Apocalypse*, a World War I picture.

Valentino's most famous role was in *The Sheik* (1921). Women fell madly in love with the hero of this desert classic. The word *sheik* became slang for any man with long sideburns and slicked-down "patent leather" hair like Valentino's. The sheik's female counterpart was a *sheba*, and both were known for wild behavior.

Rudolph Valentino was a heartthrob to millions of American women. His dark features and exotic roles in the popular new movie industry set new standards of male beauty.

BEAUTY BROKERS

A new profession related to the beauty business began in the twenties. This was the professional model. In 1923, John Robert Powers, an out-of-work actor, signed up some friends and fellow actors to start the first model agency. He supplied models for professional photographers and advertising agencies. Powers recalled, "When I started…the camera was just beginning to come into use in advertising. Believing that an attractive picture could be more effective in selling than the written word, I hammered away at the idea."

Powers called himself a "broker in beauty" and looked outside the theater world for beautiful women and handsome men. Before long he signed up socialites who found modeling attractive. By 1930 the Powers Agency had a list of four hundred models, who made up to one hundred dollars a week, quite a lot for the time. Models in those days were completely responsible for their own look, applying makeup and creating their own hairstyles.

The people that Powers chose began to appear regularly in magazines that were sold throughout the country. He claimed that he chose as models, "typical American girls, pretty, healthy, vivacious, and self-reliant." He liked them to project a wholesome image, and gave them a ten-week course in grooming, posture, and diction. His agency, and others like it, further standardized the model of what was beautiful.

The "Latin lover" made several more movies, the last of them a sequel to *The Sheik* in 1926. Before it was released, Valentino suddenly died. His funeral was a mob scene. Women lined up for eleven blocks to see his body displayed. In Japan two grieving female fans committed suicide by jumping into a volcano. Bette Davis, a movie star in the 1930s, summed up Valentino's attraction: "Valentino had silently acted out the fantasies of women all over the world. Valentino and his world were a dream. A whole generation of females wanted to ride off into a sandy paradise with him."

SPORTS AND FASHION

The world of sports influenced both men's and women's clothing in the 1920s. Champions of such sports as golf, tennis, and swimming attracted fans who wanted to imitate them. Movie stars were often photographed playing sports like tennis and golf in the sunny California climate. Douglas Fairbanks and his son Doug, Jr., popularized the golf outfits of knickers (knee-length pants), patterned high socks, and heavy knit cardigan sweaters.

Tennis star Suzanne Lenglen scandalized some when she wore a short tennis dress on the court, but many other women soon adopted the fashion. All-white clothing for the sport also got its start in the twenties.

Women's bathing suits also became briefer. In 1926, Gertrude Ederle, from New York City, thrilled Americans when she became the first woman to swim the English Channel. (She also beat the men's record by nearly two hours.) She couldn't have done it in a suit from the previous decade, but Jantzen had introduced an elastic one-piece suit that bared women's legs and arms.

In the twenties, swimming was more popular than ever, and beauty contests did much to popularize a briefer bathing suit. The first Miss America contest took place in 1921 at Atlantic City, New Jersey. There were only eight finalists, all from nearby cities. The winner was Margaret Gorman from Washington, D.C. She received a trophy called the "Golden Mermaid." Even then, controversy surrounded the event. Some complained about women displaying themselves in bathing suits; others denounced the fact that Margaret had short hair.

By 1927 the number of contestants had grown to seventy-five. Organizers of the pageant tried to quell criticism by eliminating the swimsuit competition. They also announced that the winner that year, Lois Delander, did not smoke, drink tea or coffee, or even eat pickles. The competition was halted between 1928 and 1935, but ever since it has provided an indicator of American beauty. Though few winners remained well known after their year as Miss America was over, the contest enshrined the idea of the clean-cut bathing beauty as a model of attractiveness.

Paris was still a name that meant high fashion. During the 1920s, the haute couture design houses of Paris began to show their collections at fashion shows. Live models paraded before a select group of clients, wearing the new garments. A customer could choose one that she wanted made into a dress in her size. Usually, many fittings were needed and a "Paris original" was expensive enough that only the rich could afford one.

The most famous Paris designer of the era was Gabrielle "Coco" Chanel. Many have called her the most influential designer of the twentieth century. Chanel's most enduring design was the so-called "little black dress" of 1925. This would become a standard item in the wardrobe of every fashionable woman for the rest of the century. To go with it, Chanel introduced a set of black-and-white pearl earrings. This set off a rage for black-and-white matchings. She also developed a line of perfumes. The most famous scent of the century is still the one she called simply Chanel Number 5.

Chanel introduced a knitted suit in 1926 that made simple dressing fashionable. Even wealthy people now had fewer servants and wanted clothes that were easy to wear and take care of. Chanel's simple classic suits and dresses came in restrained colors that replaced the more exotic hues of the previous decade.

Chanel is also credited with starting the tanning fad. Before this time, women avoided the sun because tanned skin, associated with outdoor laborers, was regarded as lower class. But one year Chanel came back from vacation with a tan, and sunbathing became stylish. Now a tan meant that one was wealthy enough to vacation by the sea. In 1928 the haute couturier Jean Patou created the first suntan lotion. Bain de Soleil would soon follow.

When the Paris fashion shows took place in the spring of 1929, everyone noticed that hemlines had fallen. Perhaps few recalled the prediction that the stock market would go up as long as women's dresses rose. But that October, the Stock Market crashed. That set off a chain reaction that would result in the Great Depression. The 1930s would be a very different era in fashion.

7

THE GLAMOUR GIRL

In the 1930s the Great Depression threw the country into the worst crisis since the Civil War. As the demand for products fell, factories closed. Unemployed workers could not afford to buy products, and the downward economic spiral continued. Despite the hard times, Americans spent money on two related industries: movies and the beauty business.

No other medium in history had ever reached so many people as the movies. During the depression years, people went to a movie theater at least once a week. As they sat in the darkness, they watched the stars flickering larger than life on the silver screen, living in a world that was lavish and prosperous. Romantic and beautiful people such as Fred Astaire and Ginger Rogers, Katharine Hepburn, Cary Grant, Clark Gable, Marlene Dietrich, and Greta Garbo represented the dreams of a brighter future. The movies set the style tone for the decade—an era of glamour and sophistication.

The beauty business was almost depression-proof. It was probably the only industry in which new companies could start up and succeed during the 1930s. Revlon, Almay Cosmetics, and Clairol were some of the new entrants into the beauty business in this decade. All became major successes.

With nearly one fourth of all male heads of families out of work, women were told, "Don't steal a job from a man." Twenty-six states passed laws forbidding the employment of married women. Single white women were left with a limited range of low-paying jobs, such as teacher, secretary, nurse, or beautician. Black women and other minorities had even fewer opportunities. Fully one sixth of all black Americans not employed in farmwork were part of the beauty business.

For women, the 1930s look was long and sleek. Women had grown up since the 1920s. With the depression on, it was no longer possible to adopt a carefree, girlish look. Hemlines dropped, hairstyles grew longer, and curves were back in style.

The most important new fabric of the decade was nylon. It was lightweight and so strong that the DuPont Company called it "indestructible." Nylon was exhibited at the 1939 World's Fair as a "miracle yarn." As a result, expectations were high when the first stockings made of nylon appeared. DuPont arranged for them to go on sale all over the nation on May 15, 1940. Women lined up in front of stores hours before they opened. No consumer item had ever caused such excitement. As it turned out, nylon stockings were cheaper and more durable than silk, but not quite indestructible. They still developed runs and holes.

Shoes were a major fashion item in the 1930s. Heel heights varied. So did materials, which included snake, alligator, and lizard skin. The high-heeled, open-toe shoe became popular for the first time. So too did sling-back heels. Italian shoe designer Salvatore Ferragamo came to Hollywood, where he designed sandals for a production of *The Ten Commandments*. Stores started to stock his sandals, and people bought them for casual use. In 1936, Ferragamo introduced a wedge-shaped heel, and two years later, platform soles, which were very popular with women who wanted to show off their new nylons. By the end of the decade, stylish shoes were heavy and clunky. In 1939, *Vogue* magazine commented: "Nothing is dowdier than a dainty foot."

Beauty parlors thrived while other businesses closed. Women made a trip to their local parlor a weekly social event. Permanent waves and bleached hair became more common, as women sought to imitate Hollywood stars who had them.

SALVATORE FERRAGAMO

Italian shoes are traditionally among the world's best for both innovative style and quality.

The man most responsible for this reputation is Salvatore Ferragamo. Born in the tiny village of Bonito, Italy, he made his first shoes for his two sisters. Their parents were too poor to buy them shoes for their First Communion, so Salvatore borrowed leather from the cobbler to make the shoes himself. He was only nine years old. By the time he was fourteen, he had opened his own shop and had six assistants.

Ferragamo had greater ambitions and went to the United States, where he found work in Hollywood making shoes for the costume departments of movie studios. The stars who wore his shoes in the movies started to visit his Hollywood Boulevard store to buy shoes for their personal use.

He was endlessly inventive, making shoes from hummingbird feathers, tree bark, and cloth taken from chairs. Still seeking perfection, Ferragamo studied anatomy at the University of Southern California to understand the structure of the foot. He devised an arch support that made women's shoes comfortable for the first time.

In 1927, Ferragamo returned to Italy and started what became the world's most famous shoe business. His most famous style was the platform shoes made of cork, introduced during World War II. He continued to make shoes that dazzled the world of fashion until his death in 1960.

Since permanent waves took a long time, women often got manicures while they were sitting under a wave machine or dryer. Nail polish was the basis for the success of Revlon Company, founded in 1932 by Charles Revson, his brother, and Charles Lachman (the *L* in Revlon). Charles Revson knew the beauty business was about selling dreams. He put great emphasis on the colors, package designs, and advertising of his products. He offered gift packs of nail polish, tweezers, emery board, and orange stick. Revlon offered a greater variety of nail polish colors than any other company.

Max Factor, a Russian immigrant, expanded a small business into a nationwide beauty empire during the thirties. Factor had opened a wig and cosmetic shop in Los Angeles in 1908, a year after the first movie had been made there. He became the most important makeup artist in the new industry, devising new kinds of cosmetics with each development in the film industry. He patented the eyebrow pencil in 1916 and invented a lip gloss that kept actresses' lips shiny for hours.

In 1935, Factor capitalized on his experience by opening a beauty salon in Hollywood, inviting three thousand movie stars and executives to the grand opening. The salon had separate rooms for women of every hair color. Platinum-blond movie goddess Jean Harlow dedicated the "For Blondes Only" room, which had powder-blue walls. The success of the salon enabled Factor to sell his makeup products nationwide, with the powerful slogan, "Make-up for the stars—and you." Two years later, in 1937, Factor developed "pancake makeup" that would make actors and actresses look good in the brand-new Technicolor film process. It was an immediate success with the public too.

At the same time, fashion magazines such as *Vogue* and *Harper's Bazaar* (now spelled with two *a*'s) were employing the finest photographers for their picture spreads. The tradition started at *Vogue* in 1913 when Condé Nast, its owner, hired Baron Adolph de Meyer to photograph fashion spreads. Ten years later, Edward Steichen, one of the great photographers of the century, joined the staff of *Vogue*. In 1932, Steichen took the picture for *Vogue's* first photographic cover. George Hoyningen-Huene, another photographer, pioneered the outdoor fashion shoot for *Vogue*.

Harper's Bazaar entered the competition for artistic quality fashion photographs, hiring de Meyer after he left *Vogue*. Cecil Beaton, a stage set designer, created theatrical effects in his photographs of society women for *Harper's Bazaar*.

Men got their own fashion magazine with the debut of *Esquire* in 1933. Founded by Arnold Gingrich and David Smart, *Esquire* was intended to be sold in clothing stores. To attract readers, the editors published stories by well-known writers like Ernest

Hemingway. *Esquire* also featured pictures of girls, though they were painted (not photographed) by such commercial artists as Alberto Vargas and George Petty. The so-called "Petty girl" was noted for her impossibly long, slender legs, narrow waist, and prominent bust. She became a hit with men, and thus imitated by women.

The dominant influence on Americans' idea of beauty in the 1930s was, of course, Hollywood. When Dorothy Lamour wore a wraparound sarong in a movie about the South Pacific in 1935, sales of sarongs soared. The most popular prom dresses for 1939 were copies of the hoopskirt that Vivien Leigh, as Scarlett O'Hara, wore in that year's big hit *Gone With the Wind*. Because the film industry was in sunny California, movie stars wore sunglasses outside. When photographs showing them appeared in magazines and newspapers, sunglasses became a nationwide fashion accessory.

Every major film star had a certain "something" that was distinctive. In the case of Marlene Dietrich, her attractiveness depended on a thick German accent, beautiful legs, and a look that left people wondering whether she appealed more to men or to women. Her plucked eyebrows and pantsuit added to the mysterious quality she projected. Katherine Hepburn also wore pants in the movies, but her style was decidedly feminine. She often played free-spirited women who wore pants for comfort, work, and sports. Both Dietrich and Hepburn helped make pants for women acceptable, even for some kinds of evening wear.

Greta Garbo had an allure all her own. Garbo benefited from a Hollywood makeover, which emphasized her haunting eyes and high cheekbones. Directors also photographed her in soft-focus to emphasize her mysterious quality. Even though she retired in 1941 (quoting a line from one of her movies, "I vant to be alone"), she was for years afterward regarded as one of the most beautiful women of the century.

The 1930s saw the beginnings of a Hollywood—and American—type: the gorgeous bleached blonde. Jean Harlow's hair was so light that no one could think of it as natural. The tough, flirtatious, and cool characters she portrayed set a style that was imi-

❧ Greta Garbo in an MGM publicity photograph. Note the false eyelashes.

tated many times, most recently by Madonna. Movie magazines dubbed Harlow "The Blonde Bombshell."

The other great blond star of the 1930s was Mae West. Originally a stage actress, she was forty before she became a movie star. But her performances were so sexy that they were partly responsible for the demand that Hollywood censor its movies. West wrote her own scripts, which were filled with clever lines like: "It's better to be looked over than overlooked." On the screen, she liked to surround herself with younger men, like Cary Grant, and tickle the audiences with suggestive comments. In the movie *She Done Him*

Wrong (1933) she spoke one of her most famous lines: "Why don't you come up sometime and see me?" It was all in the delivery.

In silent films—where the visual image was everything—romantic male stars like Rudolph Valentino or Douglas Fairbanks had been handsome in a conventional way. With the arrival of "talkies," or movies with sound, male stars appeared who were not classically good looking at all, like Edward G. Robinson, James Cagney, and Humphrey Bogart. When Clark Gable did a screen test, the head of the studio, Jack Warner, remarked that he was too ugly even to play a mobster role. "What can you do with a guy with ears like that?" he said.

Of course, Gable's on-screen personality and infectious grin made him a romantic superstar. He became so popular that he was dubbed "the King" of Hollywood. He had an influence on men's fashions too. In the 1934 film *It Happened One Night*, he removed his shirt before going to bed. Movie audiences gasped when they saw he wore no undershirt. All over the United States, sales of men's undershirts fell drastically.

The elegance of Fred Astaire was hard for anyone to imitate. But the dancer's slender body and effortless grace charmed audiences. When he danced with Ginger Rogers, the pair radiated glamour and style that lifted the spirits of depression-era America. They lived in a world where people seemed to have no cares.

Even in real life, however, Astaire liked to dress with style. In 1923 he had appeared in a play on a London stage. The Prince of Wales—the future king Edward VIII—came backstage to congratulate him. Astaire recalled: "HRH [the prince] was unquestionably the best-dressed young man in the world, and I was missing none of it. I noted particularly the white waistcoat lapels—his own special type. This waistcoat did not show below the dress coat front. I liked that."

Astaire found out the name of the prince's tailor and went there to order a waistcoat just like the one he admired. He was politely turned away. It is a royal privilege in haute couture that the prince's clothes are made exclusively for him alone. Astaire later found an American tailor to duplicate the waistcoat.

The Prince of Wales was in fact one of the twentieth century's most important influences on men's fashions. He may be best known for devising the Windsor knot for tying a tie, and wearing the flat collar that went with this kind of tie. Today, virtually all shirt collars are that type. In the 1920s the prince popularized trousers with cuffs. His outfit for informal occasions included a peaked cap, hand-knitted Fair Isle sweater, plaids instead of tweeds, argyle socks, and "plus fours" (knickers). All these clothes were widely imitated in the United States as well as Britain.

In 1936, soon after the prince became King Edward VIII, he shocked the world by announcing he would give up the throne to marry "the woman I love." This woman was an American, Wallis Simpson, and because she was divorced he could not take her as his wife and be king. For the rest of their lives, they would be known as the duke and duchess of Windsor.

The duchess became as well known in the fashion world as her husband. She is credited with the saying, "You can neither be too thin nor too rich." So it was a surprise when the duchess chose an American designer, Mainbocher, to make her wedding dress.

The Reducomatic was the fantasy way to lose weight. You just had to slip into it, pin it shut, and then turn on the heat. A cup of water provided enough moist heat to make a wearer perspire away one to three pounds. The ads claimed that the device was also good for arthritis. Although it cost $79, a great deal of money for the time, it sold quite well. The Duke of Windsor used it.

 Women wanted to stay beautiful despite the shortages of materials during World War II. Because the military needed nylon for parachutes, nylon stockings were banned. Women mended their old stockings for as long as possible. Then many painted their legs, as this photo from 1942 shows.

Of course Mainbocher (who had been born Main Rousseau Bocher) had his design house in Paris, because that was still the center of haute couture.

Two years later, in 1939, World War II began in Europe. Germany attacked and overran France, and Paris fell under German control. In December 1941 the United States entered the conflict when Germany's ally, Japan, attacked the United States fleet at Pearl Harbor, Hawaii. The next four years would see the most destructive war in history. And it too would have an effect on fashion and style.

The War Production Board—a wartime government agency—began to set rules for civilian dress. The purpose was to make sure that no materials were wasted. The board specified the amount of fabric that could be used for garments, set the length of jackets and skirts, the widths of trouser legs, and even the number of buttons, pleats, and trimmings that could be used for outfits. For example, if a skirt was made of wool (needed for military uniforms) it could measure no more than seventy-two inches around the hem. Manufacturers of narrow skirts put a slit in them to help women walk. Suit jackets for women could be only twenty-five inches long. There was a general "no fabric on fabric" rule that eliminated cuffs, double yokes, patch pockets, and attached coat hoods.

In 1942 the War Production Board classified cosmetics as a "nonessential commodity," and sharply limited their production. The next year, however, the order was canceled. Makeup was officially recognized as essential for keeping morale high at home.

In our present-day society, with disposable everything, it is hard to comprehend the fervor for saving and reusing materials that existed during World War II. Hair salons and barbershops were asked to salvage the cut hair to be reused in making thread and rayon. J. C. Penney stores offered to reknit the holes in stockings for free. The use of elastic in bras and girdles was restricted, because it was needed for airplane and jeep tires. Metal was too precious to be used in zippers, so clothing with hooks and laces came back in style.

In military barracks, soldiers and sailors decorated their walls with photographs of beautiful women. They got the name "pinups." The serviceman's idea of beauty was fairly standard: very healthy looking girls with long legs, large buttocks and breasts, and turned-up noses.

The most famous pinups were Rita Hayworth sitting in a negligee with her feet underneath her on an unmade bed; and Betty Grable in a tight-fitting bathing suit, looking over her shoulder. A copy of the Betty Grable pinup was glued to the atomic bomb that was dropped on Hiroshima.

The "real" women (instead of the fantasy kind) were going to work. With millions of men leaving jobs to go into the armed forces, women were needed to take their places. They found that men's work outfits—such as overalls and protective hard hats—were practical. Long hair, on the other hand, was not. Veronica Lake, a movie star famous for her blond "peekaboo" hairstyle that covered one eye, publicly cut her hair. She urged other women to do the same, so that their hair would not get caught in machinery at work.

A zoot-suited boy

THE ZOOT SUIT RIOTS

Disputes over clothing have sometimes broken out into violence. Maybe the worst example of this was the so-called Zoot Suit Riots that erupted in Los Angeles in 1943.

The zoot suit featured a knee-length jacket with six-inch shoulder pads, very high-waisted trousers, usually worn with bright ties and a long dangling key chain. The zoot suit craze had begun among African Americans in Harlem in New York City and spread to Mexican Americans in Los Angeles. Sailors from the United States Navy who were stationed there started a fight with some Mexicans, and the situation escalated. Soon sailors were beating up anyone they saw wearing a zoot suit. After several days of fighting, army troops were called in to restore order.

The Office of War Information produced a film, *Glamour Girls of 1943*, that publicized the work women did on the "home front." The stereotype of the female war worker was "Rosie the Riveter," who appeared on many posters and magazine illustrations. The original "Rosie" was supposedly Rosina B. Bonavita, who (with another woman) put several thousand rivets in the wing of a fighter plane in just six hours. During the war over six million women joined Rosie in the workforce.

8

THE NEW LOOK

 Americans were grateful to the veterans returning from World War II. They had won the war, and the nation wanted to honor and reward them. Most of them needed their old jobs back again. So the women who had taken their places were hustled out to make room. Within little more than a year, four million women were fired.

For women, it was back to the home and kitchen. Women were expected to make their husbands, children, and homes the center of their lives. The man's role was to work and earn a living; the woman's role was to have dinner waiting for her husband, keep the house nice, and raise the children. And of course to make herself beautiful. A new look in fashion would soon show her the way.

A Paris designer named Christian Dior claimed that as a young man he was told by a fortune-teller, "Women are lucky for you, and through them you will achieve success." He introduced his own collection for the first time in 1947, and turned the fashion world on its ear. His designs were totally different from the styles that women had been wearing for almost two decades. An awed fashion magazine editor—Carmel Snow, of *Harper's Bazaar*—dubbed it "the New Look."

Really, it was a retro look that carried women back to the early 1900s. In contrast to the natural style of the 1930s, which followed the contours of the body, Dior sculpted an artificial sil-

Christian Dior with his New Look of 1946 put women back in longer skirts. They also had to wear more restrictive girdles to get the tiny waist his fashions favored. Many American women resented the new style as a step backward, but it prevailed. The Dior influence remained strong in the 1950s as well.

houette. His dresses featured a tiny waistline—Dior said that waists larger than seventeen inches were "repulsive"—and a full skirt that fell far below the knee. The waist required a corset, and the accent on breasts and hips meant that padding was needed in both those areas.

The New Look set off a fierce debate. Some women complained that it was not a "new" look at all, but rather a return to the old days of the corset and crinoline. When Neiman-Marcus, an expensive Texas department store, gave Christian Dior a fashion award, protesters picketed the store with signs saying: "Down With the New Look."

In the end, Dior won. The publicity given to the New Look was overwhelming, and the style caught on. Department stores sold copies of Dior's dresses for as little as twenty dollars. The New Look was the basis for women's dressy clothes for at least ten years.

Women did start to wear corsets again. The most popular was called the "Merry Widow," after a well-known operetta set in the nineteenth century. But the new corsets didn't have whalebone stays, and shortened the normal waistline by only two or three inches. (They *were* laced up very tightly and a real pain to wear for a whole evening.)

Corsets like the Merry Widow were necessary for parties, dances, and other formal occasions. At other times, most women used a bra and girdle or a panty girdle of stretchable fabric called Lastex. It had satin panels and garters to hold up the stockings.

Big breasts were highly admired as well. Bras with extra padding, pointed cups, and perfume pockets provided the proper look and fragrance. In 1958 the Maidenform company introduced a new kind of uplift bra. The ads showed a woman doing something different or exciting, dressed normally from the waist down, but wearing just a bra above. The ad copy read: "I dreamed I was a [whatever it was] in my Maidenform bra." It was one of the most famous ad campaigns of the decade.

As the 1950s began, the veterans of World War II and their families were moving to brand-new houses in suburbs. There, they would raise the largest generation in history—their children, the "baby boomers." Television antennas sprouted from every roof: The boomers would be the first generation to grow up in front of a television screen. TV provided a new and powerful advertising tool for the beauty business.

The fifties were a boom decade for cosmetics. Powder base, rouge, eye makeup, lipstick, and nail polish were now regarded as everyday products. The cosmetics industry was responsible for about 11 percent of all national advertising by 1950.

Several new companies came to the forefront of the industry. Esteé Lauder, an Austrian immigrant, had launched her company in 1946 with a face cream she had devised. Lauder started by demonstrating her products in beauty parlors and department stores. She packaged her products beautifully, and sold them at high prices, taking the risk that customers would pay. She also came up with the sales gimmick of giving a free sample or gift with each purchase. The idea was a big hit.

AFRICAN AMERICANS IN THE BEAUTY BUSINESS

African Americans carved out a larger piece of the beauty business for themselves in the postwar years. In 1945, John H. Johnson started a magazine named *Ebony*. It was the black counterpart of *Life*, and African American beauty was one of the magazine's central concerns. It ran advertisements for products that promised "lighter and brighter" skin—like Dr. Red Palmer's Skin Whitener, Nevoline, Beauty Star, and Nadinola. The makers of these products knew that to most African Americans, lighter skin promised greater popularity and success. Women in particular felt that lighter skin was attractive. Nadinola's slogan was, "Now you can be lighter than he."

In 1956, *Ebony* ran an article titled, "Lose Weight the Satchmo Way." It described the diet of orange juice and antacid laxatives used by the great jazz musician Louis "Satchmo" Armstrong. Armstrong claimed that he lost ninety-eight pounds on it in 1955. He sent a copy of the diet to President Dwight Eisenhower. In Armstrong's words, "I told the President to do it the Satchmo way and he'd feel like he's ten years old. He wrote back and said as President he isn't supposed to feel like he's ten years old."

The leading African American beauty product manufacturer was Johnson Products, founded in 1954 by George Johnson (no relation to the magazine publisher). Its first product was a hair straightener, followed by conditioners, shampoos, and a whole range of cosmetics. By the end of the 1970s, Johnson Products was the largest publicly owned company managed by African Americans.

In 1957, Esteé Lauder brought out Re-Nutric Creme, a dry-skin remedy that sold for more than $100 a jar. Other premium products at the time sold for about $10. But Lauder's ad campaign asked: "What makes a cream worth $115?" It worked. Customers believed that if it was so expensive, it must have something other creams did not. The mixture did contain both cream and costly oils such as shark oil. Whether or not it worked was up to the buyer. (They're still buying it today.)

Aiming at the other end of the market was Hazel Bishop. After the war, she launched her own lipstick company. When she approached Saks, a leading New York department store, she was told that most cosmetics salespeople in the stores were employed by the manufacturers, not by the stores. With only a single product, Bishop could not afford to hire a salesperson in every store. So she turned to less expensive stores, like drugstore chains. She got her break when the Hecht and Company store in Washington, D.C., stocked some of her lipsticks. Over six hundred sold on the first day alone. Bishop came up with a slogan: "Stays On You, Not On Him." By the end of 1950, she had sold a million lipsticks. In 1953 she sold ten million and had 25 percent of the total market.

Hazel Bishop saw clearly what the basis of the beauty business was. She said, "Anytime you come into the cosmetics industry with a product which is a success, it will be copied very quickly. . . . You must have something new and fresh to offer your customer as the competition comes in, so that you can keep one step ahead. If you change your products constantly, you can create built-in obsolescence in the industry. Change the color of your nail varnish range and whatever women have left in a bottle at home is obsolete."

Charles Revson knew about "built-in obsolescence." He had changed the colors of his lipsticks and nail polishes every year since the 1930s. In the fifties he brought out two color lines every year. But Revson surpassed Hazel Bishop (and everybody else) with his spectacular advertising campaigns. The most popular lipstick of the decade was the Revlon Company's Fire and Ice, introduced in 1952. Here is a sample of the ad copy for the Fire and Ice campaign: "What is the American Girl made of? Sugar and spice and everything nice? Not since the days of the Gibson girl! There's a New American beauty . . . she's tease and temptress, siren and gamin, dynamic and demure. Men find her slightly, delightfully baffling. Sometimes a little maddening. Yet they admit she's easily the most exciting woman in the world! She's the 1952 American Beauty, with a foolproof formula for melting a male! She's the Fire and Ice girl. (Are you?)"

Casual clothing became more important in the 1950s. Social life tended to revolve around the home and neighborhood. People had cocktail parties, played cards with their friends, or cooked on barbecues in their backyards. For these informal occasions, various kinds of pants were now acceptable clothes for women. Hip huggers, toreador pants, pedal pushers, Capri pants, and Bermuda shorts all made fashion news in the decade. (On the island of Bermuda, local laws in the 1940s forbade women from revealing their legs. So they dealt with the hot climate by copying the island's policemen, who wore knee-length shorts.)

But for any kind of business or formal occasions, pants were definitely out of bounds. Women wore dresses or skirts, often pleated, that came well below the knee. Underneath, they wore petticoats with frills of nylon net. Another skirt style was the "pencil"—a straight, often tight, style worn with a blouse or sweater.

College weekends and dances were spectacular affairs in the 1950s. The girls in this photo from a North Carolina university are at the center of homecoming celebrations. Their gowns were the typical prom dress of the time for both high school and college.

Around the home, men too adopted a more casual look. They also liked Bermuda shorts. A fad of the decade was Madras sports jackets (either made from Indian cloth or an imitation), which came in plaids that were intended to fade after the coat had been washed. For golf, which many suburban men took up, it was acceptable for men to wear colored pants and polo shirts (knit pullovers with a two- or three-button front). Men hadn't worn garments this colorful since around 1800.

In the workplace, however, men still had a "uniform." This was the gray flannel suit with matching jacket and pants pressed to a knife-edge crease. With it men wore a white shirt (only white) and conservative tie. Men always wore hats—fedoras with brims turned down in the front—and they wore hosiery that came up to just below the knee, usually held up by garters. Wing-tip shoes in a solid color, preferably black (tied with laces, not slip-ons) completed the business outfit. It signified that the man was a good provider for his family, and a reliable "company man" for the firm he worked for. As Benjamin Franklin had recommended a century and a half earlier, businessmen "dressed plainly."

The military haircuts from World War II carried over into the postwar years. Virtually all men wore their hair short, and almost none had facial hair. The crew cut, shaped almost square and made to stand up with waxy goo, became a standard male hairstyle. *Life* magazine (now a picture magazine) said in 1951 that women were excited about "common garden males…who squint through horned-rimmed glasses and whose crew cuts look as if the owner's head had just been browsed by an undecided sheep."

Women's hairstyles, on the other hand, took a bold step forward. This was the decade of blondes. In 1950 a small hairdye company named Clairol introduced the first one-step lightener and hair coloring. Five years later, a female ad executive named Shirley Polykoff came up with a phrase for a new Clairol ad campaign: "Does she…or doesn't she?" In the Clairol ads, the phrase was supposed to send the message that people couldn't really tell if you dyed your hair with Clairol. Supposedly Polykoff got the idea when her future mother-in-law asked her son, Polykoff's fiancé, the ques-

Home permanents became a beauty ritual of postwar America. The curlers shown in the picture had to be worn for many hours while different foul-smelling solutions were applied to the hair. Toni pioneered the home permanent products. The company's slogan, "Who is the girl with the natural curl and who is the girl with the Toni?" was one of the most famous ads of the 1950s.

tion in Yiddish. To emphasize the point, Clairol followed with another campaign based on the phrase: "Hair color so natural only her hairdresser knows for sure."

More women started to set their hair at home instead of going to beauty parlors. They put up their hair each night in pincurls, and later in the decade, rollers. The home permanent became popular, though its chemical stench permeated the house. The introduction of aerosol containers during World War II revolutionized hair-care products. From the 1950s onward, aerosol hair sprays were part of every fashionable woman's dressing kit. The leading product of the fifties was Helene Curtis Spray Net.

Hollywood still provided models who shaped Americans' ideas of beauty. Marilyn Monroe was the ultimate blond movie queen of the era. Much of what people saw of her on screen was manufactured by the beauty business. She had a shrewd sense of makeup and she designed her hair color, her eye makeup, her lipstick. Even her famously sexy walk was produced by the fact that she sawed a piece off the heel of one shoe. She had large breasts and a peaches-and-cream complexion—both of which were imitated (naturally or artificially) by millions of women. Yet nobody ever successfully duplicated Monroe's charm. She could convey sexiness and fun to create the image of a woman both desirable and likeable.

Other favorite blondes of the decade included Doris Day, who represented the girl next door—wholesome, wide-eyed, and pure. Cooler and more aristocratic was Grace Kelly, who became a real-life princess when she married Prince Rainier, the ruler of Monaco, in 1956 in the wedding of the decade.

Not blond but another beauty model was the pencil-thin Audrey Hepburn. Her pixie haircut, elfin face, and haute couture clothes gave her fashion chic as well as beauty. She popularized toreador pants and the balletlike Capezio shoes. *Vogue* called her in 1954, "Today's wonder girl…[who] has established a new standard of beauty." It was a standard many tried to copy. Cecil Beaton the photographer said of Audrey Hepburn: "Nobody ever looked like her before World War II…now thousands of imitations have appeared. The woods are full of emaciated young ladies with rat-nibbled hair and moon-pale faces."

Another beauty model of the fifties was not a real woman at all. She was Barbie, the amazingly popular plastic doll introduced by the Mattel Toy Company in 1959. In many ways, Barbie was a break with the past. She was no soft and cuddly baby for girls to practice mothering. She was an adult with impossibly long legs, breasts, a tiny waist, and slender hips. There have been countless variations on the Barbie doll, but for forty years little girls have grown up thinking of her as the beauty ideal.

Men too became style models in the fifties. The decade saw the beginning of the rebellious spirit that would explode in the sixties. Two movie stars, James Dean and Marlon Brando, played misfits or nonconformists who expressed that spirit. Both Dean and Brando helped to popularize the black leather jacket as the "uniform" for rebels—Brando as the leader of a motorcycle gang in the movie *The Wild One*, and Dean in *Rebel Without a Cause*. Both also wore T-shirts in their roles, restoring the undershirt to popularity. T-shirts haven't gone out of style since.

Elvis Presley led an even bigger revolution when he picked up a guitar and sang. Rock and roll had arrived, and it became the anthem of the largest generation in history. The baby boomers started to enter their teen years in the late 1950s. The term *teenager* was first used in 1953. Teenage girls shrieked when Elvis and other rock stars sang. Teenage boys, hoping for a similar reaction, tried to look like Elvis. (Another reason for doing so was that adults hated and condemned Elvis and rock and roll alike.)

THE BIRTH OF THE BLACK LEATHER JACKET

When Marlon Brando portrayed the leader of a motorcycle gang in the movie *The Wild One* in 1954, he wore a black leather jacket. Ever since, that style of jacket has been identified with motorcyclists.

The true inventor of the black leather jacket was Ross Langlitz, a mechanic for Harley-Davidson, the most famous American motorcycle manufacturer. Langlitz loved to ride motorcycles, even though he had lost a leg in an accident when he was seventeen. Like other cyclists of the time, he wore a leather jacket modeled after those worn by aircraft pilots in World War I. The leather protected against scrapes, but it was drafty, bulky, and stiff.

Langlitz decided to produce a better model. He put zippers on the sleeves and diagonally across the chest to keep the jacket from blowing up in the wind. He also made the sleeves and back longer, so that the rider could lean forward in the seat. He chose black leather only because it was less likely to show dirt. His first model went on sale for $38.50. Today his daughter still makes jackets by hand, but they cost $350 and up. Langlitz himself died in 1989, but not before he had seen his jacket become one of the most popular garments in the world.

Elvis was the first in a long line of rock-and-roll performers who became beauty models. He had long, wavy hair that was slicked down with shiny grease and turned up a little in the back. Some people thought it looked like a duck's tail, and *ducktail* is one name for the new haircut that teenage boys sported.

Teenage girls of the fifties wore full skirts with many petticoats with deep hems. Often these circle skirts were made of wool felt, with sewn-on appliqués in different motifs. The biggest rage was the "poodle skirt" with an appliqué silhouette of a poodle. A tight blouse and an elasticized belt, called a cinch belt, completed the outfit. If a girl wanted to show she was "fast," she might wear a tight skirt with a tight sweater—the tighter the better. A sporty outfit could include a sloppy joe sweater, tight Jax pants, and poppet beads. Girls wore blue jeans for informal occasions.

The most popular hairstyle was the ponytail, easy to pull back and tie up. Some girls tried poodle cuts, very short and curly, but they could require up to 125 curlers every night to get the proper effect, and needed cutting almost every two weeks. Teenage girls also liked to wear the perfect pageboy cut.

Both boys and girls looked in the bathroom mirror and found dreaded pimples sprouting. The only available remedy in the 1950s was a substance called Clearasil. It was first advertised in *Seventeen* (the first beauty magazine for teenagers) in 1951. "Clearasil works while it hides pimples amazingly!" the copy read. It was supposed to be flesh colored. It was—if your flesh happened to be orange.

In their dress and in their music, teenagers were trying to separate themselves from the adult world. But some parts of adulthood were too appealing to discard. Susan Brownmiller described the thrill teenagers felt on wearing their first pair of high heels: "To put them on and to try the first wobbly steps is to enter a new life. The forward pitch of the knees and backward thrust of the buttocks, which startles the young initiate, magically induces a leggy, stilted walk which, she will hear, is deeply provocative to behold. From this point on, whenever she puts on her heels she will be set apart from the rest of the species, children and men who walk and run and climb with natural ease." Giving up running with ease didn't seem like too much of a scarifice for a "provocative," beautiful look.

9

THE BEAUTIFUL PEOPLE

"Everything became more eccentric, more strange." That was what Polly Mellen, the fashion stylist at *Vogue*, said about the 1960s. It was a decade filled with events that were both wonderful and terrible. The nation experienced enormous changes, both good and bad. No one knew what might happen next, and the uncertainty seemed to shake people's belief in traditional standards. What had once been regarded as beautiful was no longer, and some things that had been considered ugly became beautiful.

Beauty itself—when it could be pinpointed—took on a value that was once reserved for achievement and success. Diana Vreeland, editor of *Vogue* and one of the most influential people in the world of fashion, coined the term "the Beautiful People" for those who were most favored.

Who were they? Sometimes the beautiful people came from lower-class backgrounds. Beauty was their passport to success and fame. Fame, on the other hand, was sometimes enough to make you seem beautiful. People who were definitely not beautiful by previous standards—the artist Andy Warhol, the singer Barbra Streisand, the writer Truman Capote—now were regarded as part of the beautiful people. Wealth could qualify you as a beautiful person too, if you spent your money on stylish clothing and entertained other beautiful people.

There were, of course, more serious matters going on in the sixties. The civil-rights movement, the women's liberation movement, the sexual revolution, and the anti-Vietnam War movement all shook the country in one way or another. And, not surprisingly, each of them also had an effect on beauty and the way people saw it.

The 1960s began with the election of John F. Kennedy as president. His inauguration in January 1961 brought to the White House two of the most beautiful people who ever lived there. Kennedy had the personal attraction of a movie star. He was young (the youngest man ever elected president), energetic, rich, and handsome. Young women had flocked to his campaign appearances screaming as if they were at a rock concert. The president usually appeared in public without a hat, causing the men's hat industry to practically collapse.

Kennedy's wife, Jacqueline, seemed the very model of beauty in the early years of the sixties. "Jackie," as many people called her, was the most important style setter and beauty model since the Gibson girl. She was the youngest first lady since President Grover Cleveland married twenty-two-year-old Frances Folsom in the White House in 1886.

No celebrity had more luster than she did. Women imitated her hairdo, her clothing, and her makeup. She used little powder and wore a tawny-colored lipstick. She accentuated her eyes with mascara, eyeliner, and eyebrow pencil, all expertly applied. At her husband's inauguration, she wore a "pillbox" hat that designers could hardly copy fast enough. Similarly, hairdressers quickly learned how to shape their customers' hair into the bouffant cut that Jackie favored. Her own hairdresser, Mr. Kenneth, became a celebrity.

Mrs. Kennedy displayed casual elegance by wearing beautifully cut dresses, often with no defined waistline. This released other women from the fitted silhouette of the fifties. She used few accessories—a pearl necklace, a brooch, and earrings. She wore white gloves with virtually every ensemble. She also favored low, plain shoes to de-emphasize her large feet. The exact size of them became a national guessing game. But other women were relieved that they no longer had to squeeze their feet into tiny pumps to be in fashion.

First Lady Jacqueline Kennedy was a style leader from the time she campaigned with her husband John. She popularized a new elegance. Millions of American women copied the pillbox hat she wore at the inauguration. Her bouffant hairstyle was another trendsetter.

Sales of hair spray and makeup boomed in the early 1960s. Jackie's bouffant hairstyle and the other most popular fashion—the beehive—both required artificial stiffening to stay in place. The beehive style reached heights not seen since the eighteenth century. *Newsweek*, in March 1962, described how to make a beehive: "Hold the hair straight out, tease it with a comb until it gets frizzled, then comb some of the outside hair over this big mess of frizzled-up hair. Set it in place with a cloud of hair spray." At beauty shops, women sometimes had to wear protective masks for the spraying, much as eighteenth-century ladies and men did with powdering. And as with those long-ago hairstyles, women tended to leave their beehives in place, renewing the hair spray each day.

The allure of cosmetics made a billion-dollar business out of Avon Products. Now it had a sales force of 100,000 people, mostly women, who sold door-to-door. Each "Avon lady" was trained in applying makeup. This made them more efficient salespeople than clerks in retail stores, and by the end of the decade, Avon had 20 percent of all cosmetics industry sales.

Another company of this type began in 1963—Mary Kay. The founder, Mary Kay Ash, had been a door-to-door sales person for twenty-five years. She thought she had a better way to sell products. Mary Kay representatives held parties at women's houses to put on a beauty show. Everyone got a makeup lesson and information on beauty care. Usually, the maximum number of people at the party was six, to keep the personal quality.

Mary Kay made most of her own cosmetics and sold them to the sales agents at half of what the agents charged their customers. The company offered various kinds of incentives for high-achieving sales people, such as diamond-studded bumblebee pins, the company's symbol. The best known prize was a pink Cadillac, awarded to sales agents who sold over $120,000 worth of cosmetics a year.

The upper end of the beauty business was active too. In 1962, Helena Rubinstein created her thirty-five dollar Day of Beauty. This was a salon session that began with a weigh-in, exercises, body massage, and then lunch. The afternoon included a facial, shampoo, hair styling, manicure, pedicure, and finally an expert makeup session. The pampering, luxurious six-hour "day" was very popular.

At the beginning of 1964, the Beatles arrived in the United States. Their songs and style heralded what became known as the "British invasion." They wore tight-fitting Edwardian-style suits (named for England's King Edward VII, the fashion-plate son of Queen Victoria) and sported pageboy haircuts. Today, the Beatles' hairstyle looks conservative, but it enraged older Americans who thought only the crew cut was "manly." Within a year, however, it was hard to find a crew cut on any college campus in the country.

꙯ *Twiggy was the most famous model of the 1960s and the first model to become a genuine superstar. She was part of the British invasion and a symbol of "swinging London." Many people made fun of her extreme thinness, but the look became popular and remains so to this day.*

Before long, the British influence crept into all areas of fashion. Other British rockers appeared, such as the Rolling Stones and the Who. American teenagers loved the music, and also saw that the British invaders wore new and different clothing. Many of the British rockers shopped on Carnaby Street, a street in London where young designers had opened shops. Their style was generally known as "Mod," short, of course, for modern.

The best known of the new British designers was Mary Quant. In the early sixties, she introduced the miniskirt, which came to eight or nine inches above the knee. For anyone to wear it, a new kind of undergarment had to be invented: panty hose, which showed off legs, but without garters.

Quant herself realized that the "look" of the sixties had to be youthful. She said, "Makeup old-style is out. It is used as expertly as ever, but it is not designed to show. The ideal now is to look as if you have a baby skin untouched by cosmetics. Lipstick is kept to a pale gloss and the only area where you can go to town is around the eyes. There you can use the lot . . . eyeshadow, eyeliner, and lashes of mascara plus false eyelashes—even false eyebrows."

No one personified this look better than Leslie Hornby, who became a model under the name Twiggy. She was the most famous model up to this time—people who knew nothing about fashion knew her name. Many tried to copy Twiggy's exotic eye makeup. She wore three pairs of false eyelashes on the top and drew lashes underneath her eyes—just the way they were on a doll she had.

Twiggy was the forerunner of all the waiflike, broomstick-thin models of today. Resembling a boy at ninety-one pounds and with very small breasts, she started what became known as the unisex look. Her long legs, however, made her the ideal model for the miniskirt look.

The French designers were not about to let their supremacy in fashion get away without a fight. It had been Pierre Cardin who designed the Beatles' suits. Yves St. Laurent was the leader of the new French emphasis on the youthful look. He led the trend toward men's suits with two-button jackets and narrow trousers flared at the bottom (the bell-bottom look). In 1969, St.

Laurent also became the first haute couture designer to feature women's pantsuits.

In 1964, André Courrèges introduced women's outfits that included white plastic boots—something that was clearly for younger customers. He claimed he wanted to celebrate "a new sex appeal that corresponded to the young, illuminated spirit of the modern woman."

The following year Paco Rabanne introduced vinyl dresses. Later in the decade, he would make women's clothing from aluminum, linked plastic chain mail, and even from paper. He was the first Parisian designer to use African American models to display his collection. Donyale Luna, from Detroit, was his favorite. *Harper's Bazaar* at first refused to cover Rabanne's designs because of the color of the models.

Even before John F. Kennedy's assassination in 1963, there was a feeling in the air that, as singer Bob Dylan proclaimed, "the times, they are a-changin." In 1962, Helen Gurley Brown, in her widely read book *Sex and the Single Girl*, wrote: "You may marry or you may not. In today's world that is no longer the big question for women. Those who glom onto men so that they can collapse with relief, spend the rest of their days shining up their status symbol and figure they never have to reach, stretch, learn, grow, face dragons, or make a living again are the ones to be pitied. They in my opinion are the unfulfilled ones."

When Brown became editor of *Cosmopolitan* magazine three years later, she had a forum for her ideas. The magazine's sales boomed as Brown turned it into a guide to the "single girl" she had written about. The "Cosmo girl," as she came to be called, flaunted her femininity: The models featured on the cover were dressed in a more sexual manner than those in other women's magazines.

American designers and clothing manufacturers worked hard to keep up with the youth movement. Clothing showed the influence of "pop art," which took everyday images like a Campbell's soup can and turned them into icons, and op (optical) art, using geometric prints, like big black-and-white checkerboard squares, for shirts, skirts, and pants. In New York (and later San Francisco) trendy boutiques with names like Paraphernalia, Abracadabra, and Serendipity featured the latest (and shortest) dresses in the fabric of the moment.

The designer Rudi Gernreich scored a publicity coup in 1964 when he announced the "topless bathing suit." Virtually every publication in the country reported the news of this fashion "breakthrough," though few of them ran a photograph of his model Peggy Moffitt in the suit. It looked like the bottom of a standard two-piece suit with straps that crossed between the breasts and went over the shoulders. (Moffitt's eye makeup, heavy and dark, made a more lasting impact than the topless suit, which didn't catch on.)

Fashion trends changed at a breakneck pace during the sixties. It was hard to keep up. What was in one day could be out the next. The miniskirt dominated the middle of the decade, but toward the end, the maxiskirt, nearly ankle length, came in, often worn with knee-high boots. In 1969 the maxicoat fell all the way to the ankles.

Similarly, the bouffant and the beehive hairstyles dropped out of fashion after the Kennedy administration ended. Young women went for straight hair; some of them even ironed their hair to press out curls. Hair spray sales dropped, and hairstylists offered "antipermanents." For the first time, white women began buying hair straighteners.

While the Cosmo girl image freed women from certain traditional ideas, it still bound them to the idea that they had to look beautiful. And in the 1960s, one absolute necessity for being beautiful was being thin. Girls and women looked at the models in magazines and then at themselves in the mirror. The two images usually didn't match. Various kinds of crash diets became popular. In 1961 the Weight Watchers organization began. *Dr. Stillman's Quick Weight-Loss Diet*, a book published in 1967, sold over four million copies. From 1968 to 1972, the number of articles in women's magazines on diets or dieting increased by 70 percent.

The sixties were a decade of many political movements, and fashion reflected them. It was the decade of the Che Guevera look

The length of male hair was a battle line of the 1960s. Some schools forbade male students to sport long hair. This billboard from Norwalk, Connecticut, reflected the opinion of many older residents. At the time, Norwalk school officials had to appear in court to explain why four students who had been suspended because of their long hair should not be reinstated. The court ruled in favor of the students.

(beard and beret), the Mao jacket, and the Nehru jacket. The costume and look defined the hippie, the SDS radical, and the civil-rights marcher.

No look was more controversial than long hair on men, mostly young men. Schools tried to force students to cut their hair, leading to court cases over the legality of such regulations. Usually judges ruled in favor of long hair, on the grounds that it was freedom of expression. By 1970 long hair had won. There were a few diehard older men who flaunted their crew cuts, but most men, young and old, sported longer hair and sideburns.

Further out on the political spectrum were the hippies. These were young men and women who declared themselves part of the "counterculture." That is, they discarded the values of materialism that they saw as part of their parents' world. They lived in communes, both rural and urban, and tried various chemical and philosophical ways of having more meaningful lives.

Being a hippie meant dressing in a countercultural way as well. Long hair was just the beginning. Hippies adorned themselves with beads, bells, and flowers (another name for them was "flower children"). Women often wore long dresses, and the men sported work boots, jeans, and flannel shirts. Some favored sandals and Moroccan caftans. Wire-rimmed glasses ("granny glasses"), sewn-on patches with peace symbols and other signs of dissent, and bell-bottom trousers were all part of the hippie outfits.

The word *psychedelic*, originally applied to mind-altering drugs like LSD, came to have a fashion meaning as well. Anything that had swirling, bright colors on it was psychedelic. Department stores sold shirts with wild prints and pants made from bizarrely colored material, and called them hippie or psychedelic clothing. Teenagers snapped them up.

The slogan "Black Is Beautiful" first appeared in 1968. But the civil-rights movement for African Americans had been going on much longer than that. Blacks resented stereotypes in the mainstream media that portrayed them in demeaning ways. Aunt Jemima, the symbol for a brand of pancakes, was particularly disliked in the black community. When African Americans began to demonstrate for their rights in the 1960s, they took a look at the beauty issue as well.

Blacks—both male and female—had been straightening their hair for years. In the sixties, some started to let it grow and grow and grow. The "Afro" look, which surrounded the head in a halo of hair that might be a foot or more across, stood for a return to "natural" African roots. Gloria Wade Gyles wrote: "In its natural state, my hair would be a badge, a symbol of my self-esteem and racial pride." Part of the Afro look included dashikis—loose-fitting pullover shirts—and wraparound dresses and turbans. All these were made from kinte cloth, which was printed in bright African patterns.

Blacks entered the beauty business in the 1960s with a new approach: They would help black men and women look beautiful in their own ways, instead of like whites. In 1965, Flori Roberts launched a major cosmetics line for black skin. In 1969 four black

🔊 "Black Is Beautiful" was one of the slogans of the civil-rights movement of the 1960s. Many African Americans adopted a more natural hairstyle and wore African fabrics to show pride in their heritage. This family was attending Harlem's first black rodeo.

businessmen founded *Essence*, a magazine for black women who were educated and in the business world. The magazine displayed the new pride and self-awareness of black Americans.

Women in general, of all colors and backgrounds, took a new look at themselves in the 1960s. The year after Helen Gurley Brown published *Sex and the Single Girl*, another book appeared: Betty Friedan's *The Feminine Mystique*. Friedan argued that the idea of femininity that put women in the roles of mother and homemaker was wrong. She said women had given up too much in return for having their husbands go to work and make a living. Friedan's book launched what has become known as the women's liberation movement. In 1966, Friedan and other women founded the National Organization for Women (NOW).

Just as the African American civil-rights movement involved the way blacks were seen and were dressed, so did women's liberation. The ideal of beauty had always been a greater burden for women than for men. Women were "supposed" to attract men by looking beautiful. (Men could attract women by other qualities—wealth, strength, intelligence.) In the workplace, men were expected to wear certain clothing and measure up to standards of good grooming, but for a woman to get ahead, it helped if she were beautiful.

Whatever women did, people commented on their looks. *Time* magazine wrote about Gloria Steinem, another leader of NOW: "She is . . . a trim, undeniably female, blonde-streaked brunette who . . . does something for her soft suits and clinging dresses, has legs worthy of her miniskirts, and a brain that keeps conversation lively without getting tricky."

Those who supported the women's liberation movement demanded that women be accepted on the same terms as men—by how well they did their jobs, not by how good they looked. Some women came to feel that the whole idea of displaying women for their beauty was wrong.

Of course the most prominent event of this kind was the annual Miss America pageant in Atlantic City. In 1968 several busloads of women went there to picket the pageant. They set up a "Freedom Trash Can" into which they threw brassieres, *Playboy* magazines, hair curlers, and high heels. All these, they felt, turned women into sexual objects or confined them in some way that restricted their freedom.

The mainstream media (dominated by males) reacted just the way the feminists thought it would. It seized on the "bra burning" and made it a symbol of the movement. The protesters were accused of being jealous of the beautiful Miss America contestants. In the years that followed, newspapers and magazines would frequently criticize the "women's libbers" for being ugly. It was one way of not having to face their arguments.

As the sixties drew to a close, the country was divided on many issues. Fashion was one of them. The slogan of youth was "do your own thing." Even older women found that wearing pants suits and other comfortable garments was preferable to trying to imitate some beauty ideal. The beauty industry was in retreat, because it no longer could rely on women buying whatever it decided was to be the new style. Hippies didn't wear makeup. Women's libbers threw away their bras. Would other women follow their lead? Who would decide what was beautiful and what was not?

10
POWER SUITS AND DISCO WEAR

 The 1970s have been called "the Me Decade" because the idealism of the 1960s started to give way to personal concerns. It was a decade of fun, and yet it was also a time when women and African Americans made further strides toward full equality.

Women's liberation produced a definite difference between women's daytime and nighttime wear. During the day, women were concerned with "dressing for success," as the slogan ran. The women's movement had helped them to gain entry into jobs and professions, and they wanted to succeed. At night, on the other hand, the mode changed to "dressing for seduction." Out of the closet came the bright colors, bell-bottoms, and platform shoes. Night was the time for wilder makeup, with glossy lips and eyes accented with dark kohl. And—also thanks to the women's movement—it was now socially acceptable for a woman to approach the man, rather than the other way around.

Vogue described women's new freedom: "A 1970s woman can make herself a different face for each passing mood, each fantasized role, even each time of day. At the office, she can sport the fresh, 'natural' look of the career woman, by using a dozen shades and tints . . . all supposed to make her appear as if she were wearing no makeup at all. Then, in the evening she can switch to smoky mauve eye shadow and dark red lipstick touched with midnight blue, calculated to give her a mysterious aura that

Facing page: John Travolta in the movie Saturday Night Fever *created a model of male beauty in the 1970s. It was the age of disco and polyester, and Travolta as Tony Manero in the film summed up the longings of many young American men. Disco's popularity encouraged them to dress up and show their skills on the dance floor. Men were finally allowed to be peacocks, wearing clothes as colorful as women's.*

121

will . . . smite her dancing partners with an advanced case of *Saturday Night Fever.*"

Some women opted out of the beauty culture completely. They wore T-shirts, baggy pants and jeans, and didn't even shave under their arms. They were protesting against what they saw as the beauty industry's tyranny over women.

In fact, the *haute couture* fashion houses were notably unsuccessful in the seventies. They tried to dictate the length of women's hemlines one last time in 1970 with the "midi" style, in which narrow skirts fell to the middle of the calf. The midi was a bust. Women didn't want to feel hobbled again.

The following year, designers went to the other extreme and introduced "hot pants." These tight-fitting shorts looked good only on the very young or very slim—and most high-fashion customers were neither. The industry flopped for a second year in a row. For now, the high-fashion world had to wait and see what *women* wanted.

Right now, women were deciding what to wear to work. Everybody seemed to jump on the "dress for success" bandwagon. The president of the posh Fifth Avenue store Henri Bendel said, "You must look as if you're working, not playing." For the fashion industry, the success look brought a momentary boom, for the carefully tailored suits were expensive. However, they were like men's suits in another respect. They didn't go out of fashion after a season or two. They could be worn with different blouses and accessories to change their effect. So once a woman had her success wardrobe, she didn't have to buy a new one for some time. That would hurt clothing designers and manufacturers.

Cosmetics makers caught the trend too. Charles Revson of Revlon promoted a new perfume with a campaign that showed confident single working women. Revlon called the perfume Charlie. The ads showed a woman doing such independent things as signing her own checks or asking a man to dance. Within a week, stores around the country had sold out of Charlie.

With women trying to look like men (at least in the workplace), how did men respond? They adopted, for a brief time, some of the tackiest clothing of the century—polyester suits. Polyester was the name for a variety of artificial fabrics that were

DRESSING FOR SUCCESS

In the 1970's, many women were entering high positions in businesses, and others wanted to do so. In 1977, John Molloy published *The Women's Dress for Success Book*. Molloy, a former English teacher, had studied the influence of wardrobe on the careers of both men and women. He found that what women wore had an effect on the respect others gave them. To be regarded as a serious person, as a figure of authority, a woman had to dress that way. Molloy's research showed that women who dressed in business suits were more likely to feel that they were being regarded as executives, and less likely to be challenged by men.

Molloy advised women against calling attention to sexual differences in the workplace. "Dressing to succeed," he claimed, "and dressing to be sexually attractive are almost mutually exclusive. . . . Many women still cling to the conscious or unconscious belief that the only feminine way of competing is to compete as a sex object and that following fashion trends is one of the best ways to win. It's not."

Molloy's book went to the top of the best-seller lists. Women followed his advice on specific colors, fabrics, patterns, cuts, and styles of clothing. The recommended Molloy outfit was a gray or tweed suit, tailored with larger shoulders and an "unconstructed" jacket.

first used for clothing in 1953. Polyester seemed to have a lot going for it: It didn't wrinkle or crease, and could be tossed in a washing machine when it got dirty. Polyester was a knitted material, so it was easy to produce patterns and checks from it—and many manufacturers did.

In the 1970s, clothing manufacturers made polyester shirts, pants, jackets, and ties in bright colors as well as pastels of various shades. Ties grew very wide and loud in the seventies. The new style was often called "the Peacock Revolution."

Some disadvantages of polyester became apparent. The garments were hot in warm, humid weather because polyester didn't "breathe" like cotton or linen. It clung to the skin, and was also highly flammable—if a hot cigarette ash dropped on it, the polyester cloth literally melted.

Leisure suits were another attempt at fashion for males in the seventies. These had jackets that were modeled after the ones worn on big-game hunting trips. They had two breast pockets (usually with button-down flaps) and a wide belt that encircled the waist. They closed in front much higher up the chest than ordinary suits, so that their owners didn't need to wear ties. Some leisure suits were polyester as well, but most were made from cotton or other natural fibers. The fad didn't outlast the decade.

For men and women, denim was the most popular fabric of the decade. Virtually everyone wore it. Cowboys and lumberjacks—and a more numerous group of people who wanted to look like cowboys and lumberjacks—sported blue jeans made by traditional manufacturers like Levi Strauss and Lee's. Designers decided that if you can't beat 'em, join 'em, and the first designer jeans appeared.

Some designers used jeans as a springboard for full lines of clothing. One was Calvin Klein, whose ads at first showed beautiful models like Brooke Shields with the slogan "Nothing comes between me and my Calvins." Klein brought out a line of understated classic women's clothing, and would become a force in the fashion world for the next two decades.

Ralph Lauren was another American designer who rose to prominence during the seventies. Like Klein, his name eventually appeared on lines of cosmetics and other consumer items. People who didn't know anything else about fashion were aware of Calvin Klein and Ralph Lauren.

Lauren Hutton was the most successful model of the decade. She looked great in the power suit, and became the figure seen most often in Revlon's ads for Charlie perfume. In 1973, Hutton signed a $400,000 three-year contract to pose exclusively for Revlon. This compared favorably to what professional athletes were paid at the time.

Another famous model was Cheryl Tiegs. Born on a farm in Minnesota, she moved to California as a child. In the 1960s she became a teenage model. Her career took off in 1970 when she appeared in the *Sports Illustrated* issue devoted to swimsuits. (This once-

a-year issue of the magazine has become a media event, eagerly awaited by those who want to see the latest standards of beauty, and how far the editors will go in revealing them.) Tiegs signed a contract to represent Cover Girl makeup, and by 1978 had become so famous that she appeared on the cover of *Time* magazine.

Farrah Fawcett started as a fashion model but was better known as a TV star in the series *Charlie's Angels.* Tanned and physically fit, Fawcett displayed a spectacular set of teeth and a big, feathery hairdo that many young women tried to imitate. A photograph of her in a clingy bathing suit became the top pinup of the decade.

Some fashion magazines seemed to feel that you had to be blond to be beautiful, but there were some exceptions. Gia Carangi, an Italian American from Philadelphia, came to New York in the late seventies to find work as a model. Photographers loved her, even though she developed a heroin addiction. Her gaunt looks were a forerunner of the heroin chic of the nineties. She was one of the first women to die of AIDS (contracted from sharing needles).

More successful was Iman, a lithe and gorgeous African discovered by the photographer Peter Beard in 1975. To promote Iman, magazines pretended she had been born in a jungle, when in fact her father was a diplomat. In any case, by 1977 she was being paid two thousand dollars a day to pose for fashion spreads.

The seventies also saw new opportunities for African Americans in the beauty business. Black pride continued to be a powerful slogan, although the Afro declined in popularity. In 1971, Johnson Products used Swahili, an African language, to introduce a new product. "Watu Wazuri use Afro Sheen" was the slogan. It meant: "Beautiful people use Afro Sheen." In 1974, Beverly Johnson appeared on the cover of *Vogue*—the first African American to do so. By the end of the decade, Johnson broke the "cover line" in virtually all the women's magazines.

For the first time, African Americans were primary stars in major motion pictures. Diana Ross had become famous as the lead singer for the Motown group the Supremes in the 1960s. In the seventies she became a movie star, playing the tragic Billie Holliday in *Lady Sings the Blues*. Cicely Tyson, another black woman, gained critical acclaim in *Sounder*. Pam Grier starred in a series of films where she played a tough action heroine. Television too featured shows with primarily black casts, such as *Good Times* and *The Jeffersons*. There had been African American entertainers in the past, but very few had been cast in leading roles. It was significant that African Americans could now find beauty models of their own race in a mainstream movie or television show.

The market for all cosmetics grew rapidly during the seventies. Americans spent $80 million on cosmetics in 1970; by 1978 the figure was $400 million. Surveys showed that 45 percent of American women used some kind of hair coloring. Magazines publicized the "jet-setters" who followed the sun to various vacation spots. So those who couldn't afford plane tickets bought makeup and creams that made them look tanned. Teenagers were buying cosmetics at a record rate, and in 1973

126

the Bonne Bell company introduced Lip Smacker, a fruit-flavored lip gloss. The first flavor was strawberry; eventually, there were thirty-two kinds selling worldwide.

The seventies saw the emergence of new pop music styles that influenced fashions. One was "glam" or "glitter rock." Male rock stars like Mick Jagger, David Bowie, and Lou Reed painted their faces and dressed bizarrely. Elton John started his career by wearing outrageous outfits. Alice Cooper and the members of the group Kiss concealed their faces with full theatrical makeup. Pat Benatar, a female glam rocker, wore high cork platform shoes, glitter makeup, and a body stocking.

In 1972, David Bowie released an album titled "Ziggy Stardust and the Spiders From Mars." The songs were about transformations, and Bowie transformed himself into Ziggy Stardust whenever he appeared on stage. He dyed his spiked hair bright red and wore glitter makeup on his face. Soon Ziggy boys and girls were dyeing their hair in imitation. They also adopted the "rooster" hairstyle, with slicked-up spikes and a puffball in front (like a rooster's comb). Longer versions of this hairstyle were called "the shag."

Bowie and other glitter rock stars played with the idea of androgyny. Hair, clothing, and makeup would no longer indicate gender. Performers like Led Zeppelin's Robert Plant and Freddy Mercury of Queen flaunted their androgyny too. So did some women: Patti Smith and Joan Jett mimicked male bravado in their acts.

Punk rock was another seventies musical phenomenon. It began in Britain with a group called the Sex Pistols, led by a singer who named himself Johnny Rotten. They cropped their hair very short, stood it on end with Vaseline, and powdered it with talcum, much like the wig wearers of the eighteenth century used to do. Their hairstyle and ragged clothing was the inspiration of Malcolm McLaren and Vivienne Westwood, who owned a London boutique called "Too Fast to Live." Punk rock spread to America, where groups like the New York Dolls and the Ramones took up the styles. The Mohawk hairstyle, named after the Native Americans who had worn it three hundred years earlier, became popular. In the 1976 movie *Taxi Driver*, actor Robert DeNiro wore a Mohawk in his portrayal of the deranged cab driver Travis Bickle.

11

FITNESS IS EVERYTHING

The theme song for the 1980s was "The Material Girl." Madonna, who shrewdly shifted her own beauty image from year to year, sang the song. But the rest of the country seemed to be living it. Materialism and personal ambition replaced the idealism and self-sacrifice of the 1960s. In many ways, the 1980s were a repeat of the Gilded Age 1880s; flaunting one's wealth as openly as possible was the style.

Reigning over the decade were Ronald Reagan and his wife, Nancy, former movie stars who were now the president and first lady. The Reagans surrounded themselves with wealthy friends, rode horses at their California ranch, and consulted an astrologer to find out how to run the country. Nancy wore designer clothing, kept herself amazingly trim, and became a model of beauty for the "Material Wives" of the eighties.

Another of the decade's prominent women was Princess Diana, who married Prince Charles, the heir to the British throne, in 1981. Young and attractive, she charmed the world. Photographers followed her everywhere, and magazines showed their readers every designer outfit that she wore. Other young women tried to imitate her peaches-and-cream look. Because she wore hats, they came back into fashion, as did the flat shoes she wore.

In the 1980s, as in the 1880s, wealthy people were flaunting their money. In the fashion world, the best way to do this was to wear a garment that had a designer label prominently attached. The designer jeans of the seventies had started a trend. Now the names of designers were on everything from ties to T-shirts and underwear. Designers no longer produced only *haute couture* garments. Ready-to-wear clothing by Calvin Klein, Ralph Lauren, Giorgio Armani, and many others was hanging on the racks in department stores.

Women were more successful professionally than ever before. But as Naomi Wolf pointed out in her book, *The Beauty Myth*, they faced another dilemma. Although women had broken down barriers like the "religion of domesticity" of the nineteenth century and "the feminine mystique" of the 1950s, they were still defined by their appearance. To rise in the business world, they had to look good and dress for success. That was the beauty myth, and a way of keeping women in their places.

The beauty myth served the beauty business well, because it encouraged women to use more and more beauty products. Women's magazines give a boost to the beauty myth too. Although they reflect the aspirations of women in articles about successful women, they also provide unrealistic models of beauty. They stress that all their readers can be beautiful, or at least more attractive—if they spend time, energy, and especially money in pursuit of beauty. Much of the magazines' content is driven by advertising, which plays on the insecurities of women to sell products.

One example among many is the text of a Charles of the Ritz cosmetics ad: "I'm not the girl I used to be. Now I want to surround myself with beautiful things. And I want to look beautiful too. I've discovered that it's easier to face the world when I like what I see in the mirror." The message combines growing up ("not the girl") with success ("beautiful things") and looking beautiful (liking "what I see in the mirror"). The hidden message is that if you *don't* like what you see in the mirror, you're not successful.

The beauty myth was not imaginary. In 1983, Christine Craft, a former TV anchor, brought a lawsuit against a TV station that had fired her. Craft claimed that she had been told she was "too old, too unattractive, and not deferential to men." Craft was thirty-six, and by most standards quite attractive. But the standards of television were even higher. She testified that she had been forced to undergo makeovers and to wear clothing picked out by her bosses. She was given a day-to-day chart of clothing that she had to wear and pay for. No male broadcasters were treated this way. Two juries decided that Craft's complaint was justified and ruled in her favor. But a (male) judge overturned their verdicts. In the end, Craft was blacklisted from the TV news business.

Businesswomen retained the trim, conservative suits that they had adopted. A simple necklace or pin was enough jewelry. The only permissible color in the businesswoman's outfit was a fancy silk scarf. The most expensive ones were made by Hermés, but there were plenty of imitators.

It may have been a suppressed desire for frilliness and frivolity that drove one of the beauty business's hottest retailing trends in the eighties. This was Victoria's Secret, both a chain of stores and a mail-order catalog that seemed to appear in millions of mailboxes at least once a week. Victoria's Secret specialized in sexy lingerie, but it was the sizzle surrounding it that sold the lingerie.

The decor in Victoria's Secret stores and the beautiful models in its catalogs hinted at the style of a fancy nineteenth-century bordello. In a decade marked by sexual liberation and frankness, this should have seemed old-fashioned. But it caught on. Women were buying fancy underwear even for the office, because it gave them a feeling of femininity beneath their drab formal attire.

As the baby boomers aged, the craze for fitness and exercise increased. Jane Fonda, the movie star who had been a political radical in the sixties, promoted her exercise video in the eighties. Instead of wearing baggy shorts or sweatpants, she donned form-fitting spandex that displayed her toned body.

Spandex and Lycra were the fabrics of the eighties as people slipped into stretchy shorts and tops to ride bicycles, jog, Rollerblade, or work out. Designers started to get in on the action. Norma Kamali introduced a "sweats" collection in 1981. Within two years, jog-

✑ First Lady Nancy Reagan loved designer clothes and high fashion. She brought a new sense of luxury and style to the White House. Slim and petite, she became a beauty and style model, especially for older women. Here she is seen with President Ronald Reagan and the emperor of Japan.

ging suits were on sale everywhere. These were exercise clothes that you had to be in shape to wear.

"Fitness centers" sprang up everywhere, offering more than just calisthenics and weight lifting. There were sophisticated machines designed to tone up specific parts of the body. Working for a YMCA in Tulsa in 1948, Arthur Jones was the originator of the Nautilus Time Machine. By 1980, Nautilus sales were over $20 million annually, and had many competitors, such as Nordic Track and Soloflex. By the end of the eighties, machines were priced low enough to be used in homes.

The eighties saw the nation's obsession with thinness carried to greater heights. Of course, Lycra made you look like a sausage link if you weren't thin. But the fear of obesity had other dimensions as well. Sharlene Hesse-Biber coined the term "cult of thinness" in her book *Am I Thin Enough Yet?* She wrote: "Fat is profane. To be fat is to be ugly, weak, and slovenly; to have lost control, be lazy, and have no ambition. Achieving the proper weight is not just a personal responsibility, it is a moral obligation."

Countless magazine articles told people how to be thin, emphasizing that they *should* be thin. The reasons? Personal attractiveness was the most important one. This was particularly true of women; studies showed that thin women were more self-confident. Health was another reason: The medical profession and the United States surgeon general constantly warned of the dangers of obesity, adding that as many as half of all Americans were overweight.

Models in ads and fashion spreads were invariably far thinner than the general population, giving rise to equally serious health issues: bulimia and anorexia. There is no doubt that the beauty business played a role in these disorders and in the prevalence of distorted body images among American women. A college sophomore told Sharlene Hesse-Biber: "I see commercials with these bodies and I want to look just like that. I have a collage in my room of just beautiful bodies, beautiful women. And at the bottom it says 'THIN PROMISES' in really big letters. I have it up on my mirror, so I look at it every morning, just to pump me up a little bit, motivate me, dedicate me."

꒰ Jane Fonda's Workout Record *was the start of a new career for the film actress. Her exercise record, and later videos, were part of the physical fitness movement that swept the nation in the 1980s and 90s. Millions of people used home videos like Fonda's or joined health clubs in an effort to become fit and trim.*

Both the fitness craze and the cult of thinness found an outlet in jogging, and the beauty business found a way to make money out of it. In addition to high-priced designer jogging suits, trendy runners started to wear high-priced sneakers designed for the stress of city running. It wasn't long before nonrunners discovered that running shoes were comfortable, and the shoes became popular with young and old alike. Women often wore them on the way to work, changing into heels after they arrived at the office. Cybill Shepherd wore a pair under her evening gown to the Emmy awards in 1985.

The modern running shoe was invented by University of Oregon track coach Bill Bowerman in the 1960s. He wanted his runners to have better traction, and used a waffle iron to imprint a pattern on the soles of ordinary sneakers. He named the product Nike, after the Greek goddess of victory. Adidas and many competitors such as New Balance and Saucony have since joined the race.

In 1984, Nike introduced its most popular model: the "Air Jordan," named after its advertising spokesman, basketball star Michael Jordan. (Nike ads incessantly chanted: "I wanna be like Mike.") Shoes like Air Jordans were popular everywhere, but no more so than among young urban black men and boys. Some commentators lamented the fact that ghetto youths would spend so much money for shoes. (About seventy-five dollars in the eighties, but the prices soon went far higher; by some newspaper accounts young men were killed by others who wanted their shoes.) Other styles originated in the ghetto and were imitated elsewhere—most importantly the "hip-hop" fashions that included very baggy pants worn extremely low on the waist.

Women runners also discovered the jogging bra, which had been invented by Hinda Miller and Lisa Lindahl at the University of Vermont. Their first version consisted of two men's athletic supporters sewn together, with the waistbands crossing in the back. Miller and Lindahl formed their own company, Jogbra, and the product took off. They became rich and sold their company to Playtex Apparel in 1990. Another running accessory that became everyday wear was the "fanny pack," a belted pouch to hold keys, money, and whatever else was usually put into purses or wallets. It seemed misnamed, for most people wore it in front, not in back.

In the beginning of the decade, glitzy makeup was fashionable. Women wore green and blue mascara on their eyelids and contrasting colors as eyeliner. After that look grew old, there was a trend to a more natural look. This brought a wave of "natural" cosmetics. The best-known marketer in this field was The Body Shop. It was a chain of stores started in England in 1976 by Anita Roddick. The stores sold only Body Shop products, which were based on natural ingredients. As the ads proclaimed, they had never been tested on animals. (Presumably, you had to find out on yourself if they were harmful.) Even the packaging of The Body Shop cosmetics was recyclable, and thus good for the planet. The stores were clean and airy, and the staff were friendly and helpful. Snobbishness was out; naturalness was in.

Other cosmetics makers sat up and took notice of The Body Shop's success. Leonard Lauder, son of Esteé, said in an interview, "By the mid-eighties, we realized something was happening in the market with consumer preferences shifting toward simplicity, toward more natural products, and overtones of Oriental thinking." The "Oriental thinking" he referred to had to do with Japan's business success in the 1980s. Anything that came from Japan or Asia (formerly known as the Orient) had to be an improvement over Western products.

Multiculturalism was another buzzword of the eighties. It was a red flag to those who felt that Americans should be all alike (as long as they looked like northern Europeans). But to others, multiculturalism reflected the richness of Americans' heritage and roots. Perhaps surprisingly, the beauty business embraced multiculturalism, particularly in its choice of fashion models. As *Vogue* commented: "Everybody's All-American. The face of American beauty has changed to reflect the nation's ethnic diversity." Such models as Paulina Porizhkova, Linda Evangelista, and Christy Turlington all had new and different looks. Of course there were other models, like Claudia Schiffer from Germany and Elle MacPherson from Australia, who fit the old stereotype of blond, blue-eyed, and Nordic.

In the eighties, models became superstars. They often became bigger than the products they were used to promote and advertise. In New York City, bars and clubs tried to attract the "hot" models to increase their business. Young girls made models objects of adoration, and saw modeling as the most glamorous of careers. Young men made pinups of them, particularly the ones who appeared in the *Sports Illustrated* swimsuit issue. The writer Jay McInerney, who published a novel about models in 1998, said: "The model's job used to be to sell clothes. And oddly enough it's become more and more about selling a notion of glamour and celebrity."

One of the decade's most influential new developments was Music Television, or MTV, which began in 1981. With more and more homes receiving cable television channels, there was now enough space on the dial to devote a whole channel to music videos. Record companies found that videos played on MTV sold records (or by the eighties, strictly speaking, CDs and tapes). In fact, if the video was appealing enough, the quality of the song really didn't matter. How the video looked became more important than the music.

Stars of MTV specialized in the unusual, the eye-catching. Prince, for example, was ambiguous in gender, as was Boy George in a totally different style. Annie Lennox of the Eurythmics adopted a masculine pose. The super tall (and crew cut) Grace Jones challenged the idea of traditional feminine looks and dress.

Madonna ("Like a Virgin") and Michael Jackson ("Thriller") were among those who became big stars because of their MTV videos—and both of them had a huge influence on fashion. Madonna combined sex appeal with humor. Her black leather jacket and brassiere, with plenty of skin showing, made fun of both male and female clothing stereotypes. Though her birth name really was Madonna (last name Ciccone) she used it to contrast the image she adopted. She wore religious symbols as decoration while projecting sexuality with the rest of her costume.

Young girls who populated the nation's shopping malls idolized Madonna. Like her, they wanted to be material girls. Madonna wannabes wore lace tank tops, tight skirts, black elbow-length fingerless gloves, spiked heels, and lots of junk jewelry. However, Madonna reinvented herself with each new album, sending her devotees back to the stores for new outfits.

Michael Jackson had been the youngest and cutest of The Jackson Five, a Motown group of the seventies. In the eighties he emerged as a solo performer, his voice still a boyish soprano, but he had lighter skin and curly hair instead of a bushy Afro. He developed a new sliding-step dance called the Moonwalk, and in his MTV videos he wore a fedora hat and one glove covered with rhinestones. Glovemania among teenagers took off after the 1984

Madonna sang about being the "Material Girl"—an appropriate anthem for the materialistic 1980s. Here she appears in her movie Desperately Seeking Susan, *where her outfit was a peculiar throwing together of different fashion elements that Madonna made her own. Many young girls sought to copy Madonna's consciously trashy look.*

Grammy Awards. Jackson won eight Grammies, and on each trip to the stage he displayed the glove that was said to have 1,200 Austrian crystal rhinestones, which it took a seamstress more than 40 hours to sew on.

Jackson, like Madonna, went through many transformations, combining elements of child and adult, male and female, and even white and black. He had the rims of his eyes tattooed as a permanent eyeliner, and underwent many plastic surgeries to change his looks. His popularity was worldwide; virtually everywhere he appeared he was surrounded by crowds. Few people imitated his extreme efforts to change his looks, but the idea that you could become virtually anything you wanted was appealing, in a way.

MTV's fast-paced, vivid-image style crossed over into network television with the debut of the detective series *Miami Vice*. The two stars, Don Johnson and Philip Michael Thomas, projected the ultimate in cool and wore clothing that created fashion trends among men. Johnson sported a white sports coat over pastel-colored T-shirts, a look that swept the country. Thomas wore sharkskin double-breasted suits that clung to his body. For a time men tried that look to see if it made them resemble the trim and muscular Thomas. (It did only if they spent hours on a Nautilus machine.)

12

EVERYONE CAN BE BEAUTIFUL

 Walking down the streets of any large American city in the late 1990s, you could see an endless variety of fashions. Some women might be wearing dresses to their ankles; others chose miniskirts that went above their knees. Many had solved the business-suit problem by dressing entirely in black, with a jacket over either skirt or pants. A plain blouse in white, with a touch of color added by a scarf or pin, completed the outfit. Men too wore a great many kinds of outfits—everything from pin-striped business suits to brightly colored slacks and polo shirts. Offices adopted "casual days" when employees could wear whatever was comfortable.

Young people carried the style display even further. Boys were fond of huge baggy pants and jeans, worn far below the waist. Some girls imitated the baggy, boyish look so that their hips disappeared beneath shapeless cloth. Other girls, by contrast, wore jeans so tight that they looked sprayed on. Both sexes pierced their bodies (as well as their ears) with jewelry, sported tattoos, and displayed their underwear as part of their everyday outfits.

It would be wrong to conclude from this diversity of styles that fashion itself had gone . . . out of fashion. What seemed to be the case was that there were many fashions. As the American designer Betsey Johnson said, "I like personal dressing, anything and everything as long as you're happy." People wore what pleased them, what suited their own taste, and perhaps what fulfilled their own visions of who they were.

Now, if you had enough money and time, you could change nearly everything about your physical appearance. Cosmetic surgery had advanced so much that it could give people an entirely new look from their eyebrows to their toes. Hormones could now be injected into people's bodies to produce a more youthful appearance. And genetics, a science that promised to change all living things in ways as yet unforeseen, could be used to produce a world of beautiful people—soon, if not now.

Not that people had abandoned the old ways of enhancing their beauty. Cosmetics sales had never been so brisk. The latest retailing trend was stores devoted entirely to cosmetics. Some, like Origins, Garden Botanica, and Makeup Forever, sold only one brand. One of the newest examples of this marketing trend is 5S, which sells Shiseido products. Shiseido, a Japanese company that is the third-largest cosmetics firm in the world, started in 1872 as a pharmacy. It began marketing its line of cosmetics outside Japan in 1957. Today, with more than six hundred products, it is opening 5S stores in the United States. Inside, customers can move from counter to counter, sampling products with the help of the store's personnel. A bulletin board gives people space to post their own personal beauty tips. The atmosphere is relaxed and friendly.

A French retailer developed the idea of selling many brands of cosmetics under one roof, where the salespeople work for the store, not the cosmetics maker. The stores, named Sephora, are glass-and-chrome supermarkets where shoppers can browse for virtually any kind of cosmetic available. There is a Sephora store in the SoHo neighborhood of Manhattan—known as the beauty district for the many cosmetics stores there—and there will soon be many more in malls throughout the country.

Another trend in cosmetics retailing was the return to old-fashioned, store-made products. Kiehl's Pharmacy in New York is an example. Founded in 1851, it still sells perfumes, homeopathic skin creams, foundation, and lip colorings. The store makes all its own products on the premises, including an "age deterrent" cream and more than three hundred other treatments for hair, body, skin, and nails. Caswell Massey, a 245-year-old pharmacy that had George Washington as a customer, still uses its old labels for its products. The owners of Caswell Massey are updating old classic prescriptions, calling them Dr. Hunter's Original Recipes (after the founder of the company).

The Body Shop gave no signs of losing its share of the cosmetics market. It came up with one of the most talked-about advertising gimmicks of the decade—their advertisements displayed an inflatable doll called Ruby. Ruby looked surprisingly like a very large Barbie doll—only Ruby was fat. The advertising copy made the message more explicit: "There are three billion women in the world, and only twelve of them look like supermodels." In other words, The Body Shop was making fun of the beauty ideals that were constantly promenaded before women from girlhood on.

However true that might have been, a lot of women still wanted to look like supermodels. The hottest selling new undergarment of the decade was the Wonderbra, which could create cleavage even for women who had small breasts. Women could also change their eye color with tinted contacts, apply lotion for an instant tan, use contouring shower and bath gels to end the "dimpled" look on skin, or take any of a variety of pills that promised, somehow, to make you thin. (At least one, a combination of two drugs known as "phen-fen," was banned because it proved to be dangerous.)

Breasts weren't the major area of concern in the nineties. Women paid more attention to their thighs and buns, in part because bathing suits were cut as high as the hips. Cellulite (fatty deposits that make the skin look rippled or bumpy) was attacked as ferociously as if it had been a deadly disease. By 1995, Americans spent more than $100 million a year on "cellulite busters"—even though all the evidence showed they didn't work.

There were things that *did* work, but they weren't cosmetic creams. Exercise was a more important part of the beauty business than ever. By the mid-nineties, fitness and health clubs were a $43 billion-dollar business. Their range of services has blossomed. Some give customers seaweed wraps (to improve skin tone) and facials. Others offer nonsurgical medical techniques such as Botox injections, chemical peels, and laser resurfacing. In Botox injections, the deadly toxin botulism is injected just under the skin to eliminate wrinkles. It numbs the area, paralyzes the muscles, and smoothes frown lines. Chemical peels and laser resurfacing burn off the upper layer of skin, or an area of damaged skin. That allows a new layer to grow in, which will, for a while, appear better than the old. Lisa Adwar, a mother and television commercial producer, commented on the reasons why she had a Botox injection: "People are living longer. We all feel young inside. Your body and face should go along with that."

If shaping your body with exercise wasn't quick enough, you could try cosmetic surgery. As one surgeon said to author Sharlene Hesse-Buber: "The technological advances in plastic surgery have allowed people to alter any part of their body within a few hours, and to literally buy a beautiful face or body." In the nineties, cosmetic surgery became quicker and more affordable than ever. Chains of clinics sprang up where surgeons specialized in one kind of operation, and could do it at bargain prices. Face-lifts could be done in an hour or two.

The most popular new body-shaping method of the decade was liposuction. In this procedure, the doctor injected a narrow tube into a fatty portion of the body. The fat was literally sucked out. Thighs, upper arms, and buttocks could be shrunk in an afternoon. (Reports that once in a while liposuction resulted in serious infections or even death didn't deter beauty seekers from offering up their flesh for the surgeon's tool.) For the first time in history, a person could choose to make a part of their body thinner. By far the most popular part was the thigh. A 1993 survey reported that 72 percent of women interviewed wanted "better thighs," while only 6 percent wanted "better breasts."

The breast may have been less important to many women's beauty image, but it wasn't forgotten. Silicone breast implants, which had become popular in the 1970s, were halted in 1992 because of medical problems associated with them. Two years later, three companies that had made the implants paid a settlement of $3.7 billion to women who had suffered from their implants. Women weren't scared off from getting breast enhancement surgery by other methods—the number of such procedures more than tripled between 1992 and 1997. However, a sizable group of women (and some men!) went in the other direction, choosing breast *reduction* treatments to achieve a slimmer look.

Some people, attracted by the possibility of a complete makeover, made cosmetic surgery a way of life. The public was fascinated with Cindy Jackson, who declared it her goal to look just like the Barbie doll. By 1998, Jackson had spent over $100,000 on 27 separate cosmetic procedures in her pursuit of Barbieness. Among other things that surgeons did to her was saw through her jawbone and reset it to make her chin less prominent. Jackson said in a TV interview that she would continue to have surgeries to prevent her looks from aging.

The singer Michael Jackson was another well-publicized case. He changed virtually everything about his face, including skin color. (He claimed that the lightening of his skin was the result of a disease.) His nose shrank to almost nothing, and even his eyes seemed different, possibly due to the eyeliner tattoos he had. Most people felt that what Michael Jackson had done to himself was certainly not an improvement. He was an example of someone not knowing when to stop.

Science itself may not know how far is too far in the pursuit of beauty. The most publicized attempt to find the fountain of youth in the 1990s was human growth hormone, or HGH. Its fans claim that it gives glowing skin, increases muscle tone and mass, speeds up metabolism, heightens mental sharpness and sex drive. Originally it was developed to treat children who did not grow properly; now it is touted as a drug to stop or even reverse aging. Doctors who promote it claim that it builds muscle, firms skin, redistributes body fat, and enhances memory.

Government scientists disagree; they say they have found no proof of these supposed benefits. Instead, there may be unfavorable side effects such as swollen ankles and painful joints, diabetes,

Personal beauty is a high priority for the elderly as well as the young. Here an elderly woman gets a beauty treatment of a facial mask with cucumbers on the eyes. Many people believe that natural products like vegetables, fruits, and herbs are superior to artificial chemicals produced in a laboratory.

and high blood pressure. This has not stopped beauty-conscious people from paying $200 to $400 a week for doses of HGH.

As the baby boomers move into their fifties, they seem to have become obsessed with youth. Books such as *Reversing Human Aging, Stopping the Clock*, and *Renewal: The Anti-Aging Revolution* have been best-sellers in the nineties. Cary Cimino, interviewed at a New York sports club, said, "I used to be the hedonistic yuppie of the 1980s who was only concerned with his Mercedes-Benz. Now I'm the hedonistic yuppie of the 1990s who is only concerned about his health and well-being, and who will do anything for it."

Proponents of vitamin supplements and hormones that cost much less than HGH claim wondrous properties for their favorite substance of the month. Vitamin E, Vitamin C, Vitamin B Complex, melatonin, testosterone, enzyme Co-Q, Retin-A, and DHEA have all been in vogue at one time or another in the nineties. The available substances became a sort of alphabet soup for grown-ups. By the time this book is published, there will no doubt be more.

Some doctors condemn this trend toward self-administered youth potions. Others have turned it into a medical specialty. The

American Academy of Anti-Aging Medicine was founded in 1993. Five years later its membership numbered 4,300 doctors, specializing in the science of preserving (or restoring) youthfulness. Dr. Ronald Klatz, the president of the organization, said, "We're not about growing old gracefully. We're about *never* growing old."

The American beauty business paid more attention to non-European types in the 90s. The sensation of the modeling world in 1997 was Alek Wek, a woman from the Dinka tribe of Sudan. Five feet eleven inches tall, Wek had strong African features, with darker skin, natural corkscrew hair, wide nose, and full lips. Wek admitted that when she started her career, people at her modeling agency doubted that she would "sell" because her skin was too dark. But her career has taken off. When she appeared on the cover of *Elle* in 1997, the magazine was flooded with appreciative letters.

Some African Americans feel that buying African clothing gives them a stronger connection with their roots. Mud cloth suits (the term comes from the mud dyes used for coloring) can be seen in large cities with substantial African American populations. Michel Marriott, writing in the *New York Times*, explained the feeling of trying on such a suit: "The weight and regal cut of the cloth made me feel, well, reconnected. It made me feel like the sankofa symbol, a design often found on African fabrics. It is a bird craning its head back, suggesting that you must look into the past to go into the future."

The major cosmetics companies have also introduced products aimed specifically at African Americans. Revlon, Clinique, Cover Girl, Maybelline, Prescriptives, and M.A.C. offer specialty lines such as Black Opal, All Skins, Shades of You, and Interface. However, Mikki Taylor, the beauty editor for *Essence*, points out that there is still not a wide enough range of beauty products for black women. "There are some [women] who will find a foundation or powder in one line and others who cannot. Women who have very deep skin tone still have to make a search for a product that matches. In 1998, you think that makeup should be a no-brainer for everyone. For women of color, it's still not there."

Ethnic beauty salons are showing up everywhere, from New York to Los Angeles. As the fastest growing ethnic group, Latinos have become important to the beauty business. Physically, Latinos run the whole gamut of skin types from very light to very dark, and face the same makeup problems as African Americans. The center of the Hispanic American beauty world is Miami, where an influx of Cuban immigrants paved the way for newcomers from all over Latin America. Samy Suarez is the owner of Samy Salon Systems of Miami, where hot Latin music is served along with strong Cuban coffee. Suarez feels that it takes a special approach to please Latinos. "Unlike most Anglo women—who want to be in and out of the salon in a flash—my Latin customers love to be pampered," he says. "The sophisticated Hispanic woman in Miami likes long, stylized hair, sexy upsweeps, and thinks nothing of bringing her three-year-old daughter in for a haircut or a manicure."

The Asian American community is also becoming a significant market to the beauty business. Asians in New York are dyeing their hair in record numbers. Clairol does its testing of dyes for the Asian American market in Manhattan's Chinatown. The testers for Clairol have a hard time accommodating all the people who volunteer for a hair color change. William Leong, a student at a neighboring college, explained why he showed up: "I want to stick out, be more unique, because the typical Oriental has black hair and people think you're just into science and math."

To some Asians, dyeing one's hair can be a controversial matter, because they feel it signifies a denial of Asian heritage. Min Zhou, a sociology professor at UCLA, notes that in the past, it was unusual for Asians to dye their hair. "I think that it's not just about dyeing your hair," he says. "The symbolism is that the parents will think they are deviant, becoming bad."

But Chan Phung, an Asian American student at San Francisco State College, sees hair dyeing as a different kind of social statement: "In high school, the really badly dyed hair was how I differentiated between the cool trendy Asian party girls and the 'honors and AP kids,' who usually stuck to their natural tresses. Recently, I've been seeing a lot of flame red Asians, and really

really light blond ones. My cousin Sally now has blue hair. I guess this is just a small way of trying to be distinct and different. After all, if you're Asian, isn't the one predetermined trait the characteristic black hair?"

The Native American fashion of tattooing became a craze among young Americans of the nineties. Particularly popular tattoos were upper-arm bands, anklets, and small flowers. However, tattoo artists have created more elaborate designs and incorporated new styles from all over the world.

Although tattoos can be removed with laser treatments, tattooing generally is regarded as a permanent process. So by the late nineties some people choose henna-paint designs instead. The art

A NINETIES SUCCESS STORY

Dineh Mohajer showed that individuals can still enter the beauty business with a splash. The daughter of an Iranian-born doctor, Dineh worked at Fred Segal, a Los Angeles boutique. In 1995 she fell in love with a pair of blue Dolce and Gabbana sandals, and decided she needed matching nail polish. With her boyfriend and sister, she mixed up a batch in her bathroom. When she wore the polish, customers at the boutique noticed, so she made some sample bottles that sold like hotcakes. This being Los Angeles, some movie stars began to wear Dineh's nail polish, and then magazines mentioned it. When *Seventeen* printed her phone number, she got two thousand orders the first day.

Within two years, Dineh's company, Hard Candy cosmetics, had sales of ten million dollars. She had added products with sassy names, like Fetish eyeliner, Trailer Trash lipstick, and Psychotic lip liner. Hard Candy now has added a male line called Candy Man, with nail polishes named Testosterone, Libido, and Gigolo. Dineh's success has inspired many imitators, even among the larger cosmetics makers.

of henna painting has been popular for centuries in India and Morocco. Henna was previously used in the United States as a hair dye. Used on the body, henna fades in a month or so and the design can be replaced with something new. The hands are the traditional location, but backs and other parts of the body are decorated too.

Tattoos and body piercing are popular among younger men; most men over thirty have resisted the trend. Men in general do not like the idea of makeup. However, aftershave and colognes are acceptable, and in the nineties American men began to use hair coloring openly, especially to cover up graying hair.

Men do use cosmetic surgery and even drugs to gain more attractive bodies. A Boston plastic surgeon noted, "There is an increase in men having cosmetic surgery. . . . There is nothing more symbolic of age and infirmity and the loss of masculine vigor than for a 50-or 60-year old male to develop fatty deposits in his breasts, so that he can't go [to] the local country club pool and bare his chest. Those men are in here and having their breasts or abdomens suctioned."

Implants for males are now being used to firm up the pectoral muscles. Many of those who choose implants are bodybuilders who use cosmetic surgery to finish off what they began to attain through exercise. Gary Gordon, a bodybuilder from Oklahoma, tried calf implants when his skinny legs didn't respond to the usual calisthenics. Much like a colonial gentleman, he too wanted to have attractive calves. "It was strictly vanity and ego that made me do it," Gordon said. "But if you want to look sexier, why not?"

Body-conscious men now suffer from some of the same complexes as women do. The flip side of anorexia is called "muscle dysmorphia." This condition afflicts bodybuilders who think of themselves as ninety-eight-pound weaklings, no matter how "buff" and muscular they are in reality. For those who suffer from it, no amount of working out is enough. Some have given up their jobs so they can spend all their time in the gym. Men with dysmorphia take high doses of steroids to build bigger muscles, but they are never satisfied.

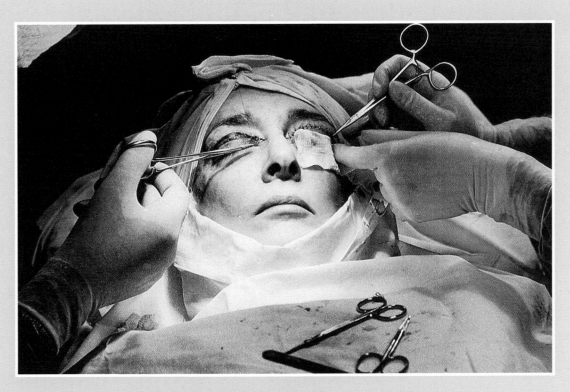

✍ *Plastic surgery has become a commonplace procedure—one of the fastest growing branches of medicine. This picture shows an eye operation. The left eye has been stitched; now stitching begins on the right, starting in the corner of the eye.*

To some, these symptoms sound absurd, but they are only an exaggerated response to the obsession with physical appearance that is so characteristic of American society. Men are only now catching up with women in the concern for personal beauty, but the response is the same.

As a new millennium dawned, what lay ahead for the beauty business? More growth and success seemed likely, for the pursuit of beauty had never been stronger. Images of beautiful people are constantly thrust in front of us through billboards, television, movies, and magazines. So we constantly appraise our own faces and bodies, comparing them with perfect looks. Confronted with the

KATE MOSS

It was a success story to excite the imagination of teenage girls everywhere. Kate Moss, a fourteen-year-old English tourist, was waiting at New York's JFK airport for her flight back home. There was an airline strike, and she had to wait at the airport for three days—a nightmare for any traveler. While there, however, she was spotted by Sarah Doukas, the head of a modeling agency. From that chance meeting, Kate became one of the world's most famous models.

Kate didn't seem like the model type. She was short for a model, five feet seven, and didn't have the gorgeous face that usually grabs people's attention. What she did have was an ever-present pout and a remarkably thin body. Some accused the magazines that splashed Kate Moss's picture across their pages of encouraging anorexia.

Moss hotly denies that she is anorexic. She says she eats normally, and just has a naturally thin body type. ("For breakfast I love eggs and bacon; for dinner, Italian food.") She admits to being a chain-smoker, something that her mother deplores.

In truth, the story of Kate Moss shows that fame is more important than good looks. Her picture was in magazines, on the sides of buses, and in endless television commercials. Her looks were unusual enough to make her recognizable, and fashion designer Calvin Klein decided to build his extensive ad campaigns around her. Kate Moss became famous because everybody already knew who she was—and also because she never smiled. Keep that in mind the next time you're hanging out at the airport.

most gorgeous individuals that the human race can produce, most of us feel like we don't measure up. So we buy a product that will change us, take an exercise class, pop down a pill, or do any of the other things that we think will produce a more beautiful person. Some people go further—having operations or damaging their health with eating disorders.

Surveys have shown that young girls today are obsessed with their bodies and looks. Losing weight and attaining beauty are the highest goals—way before character and success in school. Even women who have accomplishments to their credit are evaluated on their looks. Hillary Rodham Clinton, a graduate of Yale Law School and a successful attorney, faced constant criticism of her hairstyle and looks during her husband's 1992 campaign for president. The media felt that her physical image was far more important than her intellectual achievements.

Most frightening of all are the possibilities opened up by the science of genetics. Already, scientists are improving plants and animals by altering their genetic code. Gene therapy has helped people to avoid or identify diseases. But in the future, the science may make it possible to improve people's looks. What kind of society will result?

We can predict that the number of blondes will increase, because the blond color is already the most popular hair dye (as well as the most popular Barbie). The number-one contact lens color is blue, so eyes of the genetically produced population will be predominantly blue. Tall, muscular men and petite women, both sexes slim and yet shapely—this may yet be the look of the future. But it is almost certain that the beauty business will always find ways to convince us that some people look better than others, and that this cream or that lotion or those clothes will make us, like the witch in *Snow White*, "the fairest of them all."

SOURCE NOTES

page 7: Friday, Nancy, *The Power of Beauty* (New York: HarperCollins, 1996), 2.

page 8: Ibid., 48.

page 9: Hall, Lee, *Common Threads: A Parade of American Clothing* (Boston: Little, Brown, 1992), 6.

page 11, top: Wecter, Dixon, *The Saga of American Society* (New York: Scribner's, 1970), 21.

page 11, bottom: Baker, Patricia, *Fashions of a Decade: The '50s* (New York: Facts On File, 1995), 43.

page 12: Severn, Bill, *The Long and Short of It: Five Thousand Years of Fun and Folly Over Hair* (New York: David McKay, 1971), 50.

page 13: Ibid., 52.

page 14: Editors of Reader's Digest, *Discovering America's Past* (Pleasantville, NY: The Reader's Digest Association, 1993), 128.

page 16: Schnurnberger, Lynn, *Let There Be Clothes: 40,000 Years of Fashion* (New York: Workman, 1991), 190.

page 20: Schwartz, Hillel, *Never Satisfied: A Cultural History of Diets, Fantasies, and Fat* (New York: The Free Press, 1986), 14.

page 21: Woloch, Nancy, *Women and the American Experience*, Vol. 1, 2nd edition (New York: McGraw-Hill, 1994), 80.

page 22: Earle, Alice Morse, *Costumes of Colonial Times* (New York: Empire State Book Co., 1924), 65.

page 23: Earle, Alice Morse, *Two Centuries of Costume in America, 1620 -1820*, Vol. 2 (New York, Macmillan, 1903), 513-514.

page 25, top: Schnurnberger, Op. Cit., 228.

page 25, bottom: Kerber, Linda K., *Women of the Republic: Intellect and Ideology in Revolutionary America* (New York: W. W. Norton, 1986), 44.

page 26: Wecter, Op. Cit., 73.

page 27, top: Kerber, Op. Cit., 203-204.

page 27, bottom: DePauw, Linda, and Hunt, Conover, *"Remember the Ladies": Women in America, 1750-1815* (New York: Viking, 1976), 125.

page 28: Banner, Lois W., *American Beauty* (New York: Knopf, 1983), 39.

page 29, sidebar: Schnurnberger, Op. Cit., 257, 258, 259.

page 29, text: DePauw, Op. Cit., 118.

page 30: Weibel, Kathryn, *Mirror, Mirror: Images of Women Reflected in Popular Culture* (Garden City, NY: Anchor Press, 1977), 177.

page 32, top: Banner, Op. Cit., 45.

page 32, bottom: Ibid., 227.

page 33: Editors of *Reader's Digest*, Op. Cit., 38.

page 35, top: Banner, Op. Cit., 70.

page 35, bottom: Ibid., 234.

page 36: Ibid., 20

page 39, top: Rooks, Noliwe M., *Hair-Raising Beauty, Culture, and African American Women* (New Brunswick, NJ: Rutgers University Press, 1996), 37.

page 39, middle: Plante, Ellen M., *Women at Home in Victorian America: A Social History* (New York: Facts On File, 1997), 133.

page 39, bottom: Schwartz, Op. Cit., 57.

page 40: Ibid., 63.

page 41: Hall, Op. Cit., 80.

page 43: Banner, Op. Cit., 19.

page 44, top: Rooks, Op. Cit., 25.

page 44, bottom: Banner, Op. Cit., 18.

page 48, top: Ibid., 106.

page 48, middle, Ibid., 106.

page 48, bottom, Ibid., 113.

page 49: Wecter, Op. Cit., 177.

page 50: Ibid., 176.

page 53: Schnurnberger, Op. Cit., 28.

page 54: Bernikow, Louise, with the Women's History Project, *The American Women's Almanac* (New York: Berkley Books, 1997), 65.

page 57: Banner, Op. Cit., 103-104.

page 59: Ibid., 150.

page 60: Schwartz, Op. Cit., 89.

page 61: Ernst, Robert, *Weakness Is a Crime: The Life of Bernarr MacFadden* (Syracuse, NY: Syracuse University Press, 1991), 21.

page 65: Schwartz, Op. Cit., 92.

page 69: Rubinstein, Helena, *My Life for Beauty* (New York: Simon & Schuster, 1966), 14.

page 70: *Ibid.*, 57-58.

page 76, top: Severn, Op. Cit., 122.

page 76, bottom: Ibid., 124.

page 81, sidebar left: Leach, William, *Land of Desire: Merchants, Power, and the Rise of a New American Culture* (New York: Vintage Books, 1994), 309.

page 81, sidebar right: Ibid., 310.

page 85: Schnurnberger, Op. Cit., 358.

page 89: Editors of *Reader's Digest*, Op. Cit., 202.

page 90, top: Boardman, Barrington, *Flappers, Bootleggers, "Typhoid Mary," and the Bomb: An Anecdotal History of the United States from 1923-1945* (New York, Harper Perennial Library, 1989), 156.

page 90, middle, Ibid., 119.

page 90, bottom: Herald, Jacqueline, *Fashions of a Decade: The 1920s* (New York: Facts On File, 1997), 33.

page 96: Schnurnberger, Op. Cit., 366.

page 99, sidebar: Schwartz, Op. Cit., 250.

page 100, top: Allen, Margaret, *Selling Dreams: Inside the Beauty Business* (New York: Simon & Schuster, 1981), 52.

page 100, bottom: De Castelbajac, Kate, *The Face of the Century: 100 Years of Makeup and Style* (New York: Rizzoli, 1995), 115.

page 102: Severn, Op. Cit., 127.

page 103: *The New York Times*, June 8, 1998, B12.

page 104: De Castelbajac, Op. Cit., 123.

page 106: Marwick, Arthur, *Beauty in History* (London: Thames and Hudson, 1988), 29.

page 107: Gross, Michael, *Model: The Ugly Business of Beautiful Women* (New York: Warner Books, 1996), 250.

page 110: Severn, Op. Cit., 130.

page 112: De Castelbajac, Op. Cit., 130.

page 113: Douglas, Susan J., *Where the Girls Are: Growing Up Female With the Mass Media* (New York: Times Books, 1995), 69.

page 116: Rooks, Op. Cit., 6-7.

page 118: Friday, Op. Cit., 333-334.

page 121: De Castelbajac, Op. Cit., 148.

page 122: Faludi, Susan, *Backlash: The Undeclared War Against American Women* (New York: Crown, 1991), 174.

page 123, sidebar: Ibid., 175.

page 126: Rooks, Op. Cit., 129.

page 131, top: Douglas, Op. Cit., 245.

page 131, bottom: Wolf, Naomi, *The Beauty Myth* (New York: Anchor Books, 1992), 35.

page 134, top: Hesse-Biber, Sharlene, *Am I Thin Enough Yet? The Cult of Thinness and the Commercialization of Identity* (New York: Oxford University Press, 1996), 11.

page 134, bottom: Ibid., 59.

page 137, top: De Castelbajac, Op. Cit., 178.

page 137, middle: Peiss, Kathy, *Hope in a Jar: The Making of America's Beauty Culture* (New York: Metropolitan Books, Henry Holt and Co., 1998), 263.

page 137, bottom: *The New York Times*, July 12, 1998, Section 9: 1, 5.

page 141: Feldman, Elaine, *Fashions of a Decade: The 1990s* (New York: Facts On File, 1992), 25.

page 144, top: *The New York Times*, May 17,1998, Section 9: 5.

page 144, bottom: Douglas, Op. Cit., 263.

page 146: *The New York Times*, April 12, 1998, Section 9: 1-2.

page 147, top: *The New York Times*, October 26, 1997, Section 9: 5.

page 147, bottom: *The New York Times*, April 12, 1998, Section 9: 2.

page 148, Suarez: *Vogue*, June, 1993, p.130.

page 148, Leong: *The New York Times*, October 26,1997, Section 9: 3.

page 148, Zhou: Ibid., 3.

page 148, Phung: author interview.

page 150, top: Hesse-Biber, Op. Cit., 96.

page 150, bottom: Editors of Time-Life Books, *All the Rage* (Alexandria, VA: Time-Life Books, 1992), 11.

page 152: *Vanity Fair*, January 1994, 56.

INDEX

Page numbers in *italics* refer
to illustrations.

advertising, 45–46, 54, 68, 98, 100
African Americans, 38–39, 50, 70, 85,
    99, 113, 116, *117*, 118, 126, 147
Afro look, 116, 126
androgyny, 127
Arden, Elizabeth, 68–70
Asian Americans, 148–149
Astaire, Fred, 90
Atlas, Charles (Angelo Siciliano), 78–
    79
Avon Products, 50, 110
Ayer, Harriet Hubbard, 48, 50, 62

Banting, William, 66
Bara, Theda, 68
barbershops, 55, *61*
Barbie doll, 104, 145
beards, 55
Beatles, the, 111
Beaton, Cecil, 104
beauty contests, 82–83, 118–119
beauty patches, *19*, 19–20, 30
Bedell, Grace, 55
Beecher, Catherine, 35
Bermuda shorts, 101, 102
bicycling, 62, *63*
Bishop, Hazel, 100
Bloomer, Amelia Jenks, 40–42
bloomers, 41, *42*, 63
blue jeans, 124
body piercing, 10, 141, 150
Body Shop, 136–137, 143
bombast, 10

Bonavita, Rosina B., 95
bosom bottles, 17
bosom friend, 15
Bow, Clara, 79
Bowie, David, 127, *128*
Brady, Diamond Jim, 54, 55
Brady, Matthew, 47, 54
Brando, Marlon, 104–105
brassieres, 74, 98, 136, 143
breast enhancement surgery, 146
Brooks, Henry Sands, 37
Brooks Brothers, 35, 37
Brown, Helen Gurley, 113
Brown, Henry Collins, 66
Brownmiller, Susan, 106
Burberry, Thomas, 71
bustles, 47–48, *48*
Butterick, Charles, 52, 54
Byron, Lord, 32–33

calico cloth, 26
Carangi, Gia, 125
Cardin, Pierre, 112
Castle, Irene, 67, 71
Castle, Vernon, 67
Caswell-Massey Company, 17, 143
cellulite, 143
Chanel, Gabrielle "Coco," 83
Chap Stick, 52
Che Guevera look, 114–115
Chesebrough, Robert A., 50
Christy, Howard Chandler, 71
Christy girl, 71
civil-rights movement, 116, 118
Civil War, 45, 47
Clairol, 102–103

Clinton, Hillary Rodham, 153
Cody, Buffalo Bill, 54
Colonial America, 9–22
commode, 14
corsets, 8, 14–15, 27, 28, 31, 38, 40,
    47–48, 59, 65, 71, 97–98
cosmetics, 16–17, 30, 39, 50, 51, 52,
    68–70, 76, 78, 84, 87, 93, 98–100,
    110–111, 116, 126–127, 136–137,
    142–143, 147
cosmetic surgery, 49, 62, 142, 144, 145,
    150, 151
Cosmo girl, 113, 114
Courrèges, André, 113
Crabtree, Lotta, 46
Craft, Christine, 131–132
crinolines, 42–43, 43
cross-dressing, 18
Currier and Ives, 33
Custer, Elizabeth, 53–54

Daguerre, Louis, 45, 46
Damon, Bertha, 43
Dana, Natalie, 59
Davis, Bette, 81
Davis, Richard Harding, 60
Day, Doris, 104
Dean, James, 104–105
Demorest, Ellen Curtis, 52, 54
deodorants, 75
department stores, 36–38, 52–53
Diana, Princess, 130
Dickens, Charles, 44
dieting, 20, 39, 40, 66, 99, 114
Dietrich, Marlene, 88
Dior, Christian, 96–97, 97
disco, 129
Drinker, Elizabeth, 25

eating disorders, 66, 134, 152
Edward VIII, King of England, 90–91
Empire style, 28–29
Endicott, John, 12
exercise, 20, 39, 40, 41, 62–65, 82, 132,
    134–136, 143–144
eye makeup, 78, 87, 98, 112, 136

face powder, 30, 78
Factor, Max, 87
fashion babies, 14, 15
fashion plate, 22
Fawcett, Farrah, 125, 125
Feminine Mystique, The (Frieden), 118
Ferragamo, Salvatore, 85, 86
Field, Marshall, 52
flappers, 67, 72, 73–76, 79

Fleet, C.D., 52
Fonda, Jane, 132, 135
Foote, Abigail, 21
Foraker, Julia, 49
Franklin, Benjamin, 20, 25, 26, 102
Freeman, Martin, 38–39
French Revolution, 27
Friday, Nancy, 7, 8
Frieden, Betty, 118
fur trade, 9–10

Gable, Clark, 90
Galen, 9
Garbo, Greta, 88, 89
Garden, Mary, 76
genetics, 153
Gernreich, Rudi, 114
Gibson, Charles Dana, 59, 60
Gibson girl, 59–60, 60, 66
Gibson man, 60, 60
Gilded Age, 45
Gillette, King Camp, 60
girdles, 71
Godey's Lady's Book, 33, 34, 39, 50, 53
Grable, Betty, 94
Graham, Sylvester, 40
Great Depression, 83–85
Grecian bend, 48
Grier, Pam, 126
Gyles, Gloria Wade, 116

hair dye, 46, 68, 85, 88, 102–103, 148–
    149, 153
hair spray, 103, 110
hairstyles, 10, 11–13, 12, 23, 24, 29–30,
    38, 49, 60, 67, 75–76, 77, 85, 102–
    103, 106, 108, 109, 110, 111, 114,
    115, 115, 127
Hale, Sara Josefa, 33
Hancock, John, 22
Harland, Marion, 48
Harlow, Jean, 87–89
hats, 25, 62, 102, 108, 109, 130
Hawthorne, Nathaniel, 33
Hayworth, Rita, 94
Held, John, 72, 73, 74
hemlines, 66, 83, 85, 112, 114, 122
Hentz, Caroline Lee, 57
Hepburn, Audrey, 104
Hepburn, Katherine, 88
hippies, 115–116
hobble garter, 67
homespun clothing, 21, 26
Hooker, Joseph, 47
hoop skirt, 15, 27, 28
human growth hormone (HGH), 145–146

Hunter, William, 17
Hutton, Lauren, 124
hydropathy (water cure), 40

Iman, 126
Industrial Revolution, 31, 35
It girl, 79
Ivory soap, 52

Jackson, Andrew, 32, 33, 35
Jackson, Cindy, 145
Jackson, Michael, 138, 140, 145
Jacksonian America, 35
Jacob, Polly, 74
Jefferson, Thomas, 13
Johnson, Beverly, 126
Johnson, Don, 140

Kellogg's Corn Flakes, 66
Kelly, Grace, 104
Kemble, Frances, 32
Kennedy, Jacqueline, 108, *109*
Kennedy, John F., 108
King Tut craze, 75
Klein, Calvin, 124, 152

Lake, Veronica, 94
Lamour, Dorothy, 88
Langlitz, Ross, 105
Langtry, Lily, 46, 55
Latinos, 148
Lauder, Esteé, 98–99
Lauder, Leonard, 137
Lauren, Ralph, 124
leather jackets, 105
leg painting, 92
Leigh, Vivien, 88
Lewis, Diocletian, 40
Lincoln, Abraham, 37, 46–47, 54–55
Lincoln, Amos, 43–44
lip gloss, 87, 127
liposuction, 144, 150
lipstick, 17, 39, 68, 78, 98, 100
Longfellow, Henry Wadsworth, 33
Lorillard, Griswold, 54
Luna, Donyale, 113

Macaroni style, 21–22
Macfadden, Bernarr, 61–62, 78
Macrae, David, 39
Macy, R.H., 53
Madison, Dolley, 26
Madonna, 89, 130, 138, *139*, 140
mail-order catalogs, 53
Mainbocher, 91, 93
manicures, 49, 50, 86

Mao jacket, 115
marcelling, 67, 76
Marriot, Michel, 147
Mary Kay, 110
mascara, 50, 78
masks, 16, 26, *51*
massaging, 65
McConnell, David, 50
McInerney, Jay, 137
Mellen, Polly, 107
Menken, Ada Isaacs, 46, 55
Miller, Libby, 41
miniskirts, 112, 114
models, 81, *111*, 112, 124–126, 134, 137, 152
Moffitt, Peggy, 114
Mohajer, Dineh, 149
Mohawk hairstyle, 10, 127
Molloy, John, 123
Monroe, Marilyn, 103–104
Moss, Kate, 152
mouthwashes, 17
movies, 67–68, 79, 80, 81, 84, 88–90, 103–105, 126
MTV (Music Television), 138, 140
music, 105, 111, 127, 129, 138
mustaches, 55, 60

nail polish, 68, 86, 98, 100, 149
Napoleon Bonaparte, 28, 32
Native Americans, 9–10
Nehru jacket, 115
nightcaps, 13

pannier skirt, 15
Paris fashions, 83, 112–113
patterns, 52, 54
Percy, George, 9
perfumes, 17, 39, 50, 122
permanent waves, 67, 76, *77*, 85, 103, *103*
petticoat breeches, 15
petticoats, 31, 40, 101, 106
Petty girl, 88
photography, 45–47, 87
physical fitness, 20, 39, 40, *41*, 61–65, 82, 132, 134–136, 143–144
Pickford, Mary, 67–68, 71
piecework, 36
pimples, 106
pinups, 93–94, 125
plastic surgery (*see* cosmetic surgery)
plumpers, 19
Poe, Edgar Allan, 33
Poiret, Paul, 66–67
polyester suits, 122–124

pomanders, 17
Pond, Theron, 39
Pory, John, 11
powder room, 13
Powers, John Robert, 81
power suits, 122–124
Presley, Elvis, 105, 106
Procter and Gamble, 52
prom dresses, *101*
prostitution, 47
pumpkin breeches, 10
Puritans, 11, 12

Quant, Mary, 112

Rabanne, Paco, 113
razors, 60
ready-to-wear clothing,
    introduction of, 35
Reagan, Nancy, 130, *133*
Reagan, Ronald, 130, *133*
Revlon Company, 86, 100, 122, 124
Revolutionary period, 21, 23, 25–27
Roe, John Orlando, 49
Roebuck, Alvah, 53
Rogers, Ginger, 90
Rosenthal, Ida Cohen, 74
Ross, Diana, 126
rouge, 17, 30, 39, 68, 78, 98
Royall, Anne, 36
Rubinstein, Helena, 69–70, 110–111
RuPaul, 18
Rush, Benjamin, 27
Russell, Lillian, 46, 55, 56, *64–65*

St. Laurent, Yves, 112–113
Sala, George, 35
sanitary napkins, 71
sans culottes, 27
Sears, Richard, 53
sewing machines, 36, 52
Shields, Brooke, 124
shirtwaist, 58–60
shoes, 15–16, 47, 53, 85, 86, 102, 106,
    108, 129, 130, 135–136
silicone breast implants, 144–145
Simpson, Wallis, 91
slavery, 39, 40, 43–44
smallpox, 19
sneakers, 53, 135–136
soap, 30, 45
spas, 40
Stanton, Elizabeth Cady, 41
Steinem, Gloria, 118

stockings, 75, 85
stomacher, 15
Stowe, Harriet Beecher, 33, 40
Sullivan, John L., 54
sumptuary laws, 11
sunbathing, 83
swimsuits, 63–64, *64*, 82, 114

Taft, William Howard, 60–61
tape measure, invention of, 35
tattooing, 10, 141, 149–150
Taylor, Mikki, 147
Thomas, Philip Michael, 140
Tiegs, Cheryl, 124–125
Tilghman, Molly, 27
Tomes, Robert, 48–49
tooth care, 17
Travolta, John, *120*, 121, 129
tuxedo, 54
Twiggy, *111*, 112
Tyson, Cicely, 126

unisex look, 112

Valentino, Rudolph, 79, *80*, 81
Van Buren, Martin, 36
Vaseline, 50
Victoria's Secret, 132
vitamins, 146
Vreeland, Diana, 107

Walker, Madam C.J., 70
Ward, Aaron Montgomery, 53
Warren, J. Mason, 49
Washington, George, 16, 25, 26, 143
Washington, Martha, 14, 16, 26
weight, 48, 60–61, 64–66, 78, 112, 152
Weir, Robert Fulton, 49
Wek, Alek, 147
West, Mae, 89–90
whalebone stays, 14, 15, 32
wigs, 13–14, 27, 30
Winslow, Anna Green, 23
Wolf, Naomi, 131
women's liberation, 58, 118–119, 121
women's suffrage, 58
working women, 58, 59, 94–95
World War I, 71
World War II, 93–95
Worth, Charles, 48

Young, Brigham, 41

Zoot Suit Riots, 94